PLACEHOLDER FOR OUTSIDE COVER PAGE

-DISCARD ONCE PRINTED-

Contact Us!

Giggle nook Publications
Math with a Smile

Dr. Nicki Newton
Email: gigglenook@gmail.com
Website: www.drnicki123.com
Blog: guidedmath.wordpress.com

Also by Dr. Nicki Newton

Guided Math in Action: Building Math Proficiency
Problem Solving With Math Models: Grade K
Problem Solving With Math Models: Grade 1
Problem Solving With Math Models: Grade 3
Problem Solving With Math Models: Grade 4
Problem Solving With Math Models: Grade 5

PROBLEM SOLVING™
With Math Models
Second Grade

Dr. Nicki Newton

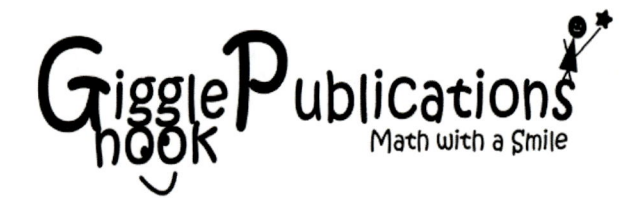

Giggle Nook Publications
Math with a Smile

Gigglenook Publication

P.O. Box 110134

Trumbull CT 06611

Email: gigglenook@gmail.com

Website: www.drnicki123.com

Produced by GiggleNook Publications
Thank you to the entire Gigglenook Production staff:

Copyright © 2012 GiggleNook Publications

All rights reserved. No part of the book may be reproduced in any form, stored in a retrieval system, by any mechanical, photocopying, recording, scanning, electronic means, or otherwise under Section 107 or 108 of the 1976 United States Copyright Act, without prior written permission in writing from the publisher, except by a reviewer, who may quote brief passages in a review. Permission is given to individual classroom teachers to reproduce the pages for classroom instruction use only. Reproduction of these materials for an entire school or district is strictly forbidden.

For additional copies of this publication or permission to reproduce this work, please contact Gigglenook.

Chief Operating Officer: Dr. Nicki Newton
Publisher: Gigglenook Publication
Cover Design: This Way Up Productions
Text Design and Composition: Bonnie Harrison-Jones

Printed in the United States of America
ISBN-13: 978-1492151517
ISBN-10: 1492151513
Volume 1: October 2013

Dedicated to Mom and Pops, Always

TABLE OF CONTENTS

Foreword	ii
Acknowledgements	iv
Introduction to the Types of Problems	1
The 2nd Grade Word Problem Standards	5
The 2nd Grade Models for Problem Solving	7
Teacher Tips	20
Unit 1 - Add To Problems	21
Unit 2 - Take From Problems	56
Unit 3 - Put Together/Take Apart Problems	91
Unit 4 - Comparison Problems	127
Unit 5 - Multi-Step Problems	166
Answer Key	191
References	198

Foreword

Story problems can be great! Story problems are the stuff life is made of. If we can make connections for children between their daily lives and the problems we pose and solve in school, we will have much more success. We need to provide scaffolds into the process.

The New Math Common Core (CCSS, 2010) places a big emphasis on problem solving. The first mathematical practice mentioned states that students should "Make sense of problems and persevere in solving them." It goes on to describe this by stating that mathematically proficient students should be able to explain a problem and find ways to enter into it. According to the New Math Common Core students should be able to solve problems with objects, drawings and equations. In this book, students will practice word problems aligned to the standards by using the CCSS designated math models.

The Math Common Core, actually adopted the framework for story problems, created by Carpenter, Fennema, Franke, Levi & Empson, 1999; Peterson, Fennema & Carpenter (1989). The research says that the more teachers understand these types of problems and teach them to their students, the better students understand the problems and are able to solve them. Furthermore, the research makes the case that the KEY WORD METHOD should be avoided! Students should learn to understand the problem types and what they are actually discussing rather than "key word" tricks. The thing about key words is that they only work with really simplistic problems and so as students do more sophisticated work with word problems, the key words do not serve them well. They may actually lead them in the wrong direction, often encouraging the wrong operation. For example, given this problem: *John has 2 apples. Kate has 3 more than he does. How many do they have altogether?* Many students just add 2 and 3 instead of unpacking the problem. Another example, given this problem: *Sue has 10 marbles. She has 2 times as many marbles as Lucy. How many marbles does Lucy have?* Often times, students just multiply because they see the word times, instead of really reading and understanding the problem.

This book is about giving students a repertoire of tools, models and strategies to help them think about, understand and solve word problems. We want to scaffold reasoning opportunities from the concrete (using objects) to the pictorial (pictures and drawings) and, finally, to the abstract (writing equations).

DR. NICKI NEWTON

ACKNOWLEDGEMENTS

I would like to thank many people for their support, expertise, guidance, and encouragement during this project. First of all, I would like to thank God, without Him this would not be possible. Second, I would like to thank my mom, pa, big mom, and granddaddy. Third, I would like to thank my family for all their love and support, especially my Tia that calls me every day and asks, "What have you accomplished today?" And finally, I would like to thank all of my friends who support me all the time. This book series would not have been possible without the continual support of the Gigglenook Production Team. Thank you all!

Introduction to the Types of Problems

Grade Specific Problem Solving Expectations

The CCSS is very specific about what students should be able to do in terms of solving word problems by grade level. There are 4 general categories for addition and subtraction problems. In kindergarten students are exposed to 4 problem types - 1 addition, 1 subtraction, and 2 part/part whole problems. They are expected to work with these types of problems through 10. But, in first grade, there is a big leap. The standards say that the children will be able to work with the above-mentioned four problems, in addition to addition and subtraction change unknown problems, the other part/ part whole problem as well as comparison problems with unknowns in all positions and with a symbol for the unknown to represent the problem through 20. Students should also be able to solve word problems with three numbers adding up to 20. By second grade, they have to be able to solve all problem types, including the harder comparison problems through 100. In 3rd through 5th grade the students should be able to solve all of the problem types using larger whole numbers, fractions and decimals.

Adding to Problems

"Adding to" problems are all about adding. There are three types. The first type is *Adding to* problems where the result is unknown. For example, *Jenny had 5 marbles. John gave her 3 more. How many marbles does Jenny have now?* In this problem the result is unknown. Teachers tend to tell these types of problems. They are basic and straightforward. The teacher should start with concrete items, then proceed to drawing out the story, then to diagramming the story, and finally to using equations to represent the story. This is the easiest type of story problem to solve.

The second kind of *Adding to* problem is the "Change Unknown" problem. For example, *Jenny had 5 marbles. John gave her some more. Now she has 8 marbles. How many marbles did John give her?* In this type of problem, the students are looking for the change. They know the start and they know the end but they don't know the *change*. So, students have to put down the start and then count up to find how many. Students could also start with 8 marbles and take away the original 5 to see how many more were added to make 8.

The third type of *Adding to* Problem is a "Start Unknown" problem. For example, *Jenny had some marbles. John gave her 3 more. Now she has 8 marbles. How many marbles did Jenny have in the beginning?* In this type of problem, the students are looking for the start. This is the hardest type of *adding to* problem to solve. This takes a great deal of modeling.

Taking From Problems

Taking From problems are all about subtracting. There are three types. The first type is *taking from* problems where the result is unknown. For example, *Jenny had 5 marbles. She gave John 3. How many marbles does Jenny have left?* In this problem, the result is unknown. Teachers tend to tell these types of problems. They are basic and straightforward. The teacher should start with concrete items, then proceed to drawing out the story, then to diagramming the story, and finally to writing equations to represent the story.

The second kind of *Taking From* problem is the "Change Unknown" problem. For example, *Jenny had 10 marbles. She gave John some. Now she has 8 marbles left. How many marbles did she give to John?* In this type of problem, the students are looking for the change. They know the start and they know the end but they don't know the *change*. So, students have to put down the start and then count up to find how many. Students could also start with 10 marbles and take away some until they have 8 left. They would count to see how many they had to take away to remain with 8.

The third type of *Taking From* problem is a "Start Unknown" problem. For example, *Jenny had some marbles. She gave John 3. Now she has 7 marbles left. How many marbles did Jenny have to start with?* In this type of problem, the students are looking for the start. This is the hardest type of *taking from* problem to solve. This takes a great deal of modeling. You can use ten frames to show this. One strategy is to have the students put down the seven she has left and count up three to see how many that makes.

Part/Part Whole Problems

A *Part/Part Whole* problem is a problem that discusses the two parts and the whole. There are three types of *Part/Part Whole* Problems. The first is a problem where the *whole* is unknown. For example, *Susie has some marbles. Five are red and five are blue. How many marbles does she have altogether?* We know both parts and the task is to figure out the whole.

The second kind of problem is a problem where one of the *parts* is unknown. For example, *Susie has 10 marbles. Seven are red. The rest are blue. How many are blue?* In this type of problem, we are given the whole and one of the parts. The task is to figure out the other part.

The third type of problem is a *Both Addends Unknown* problem. In this type of problem both addends are not known, only the total is given. For example, *There are 4 frogs on the log. Some are blue and some are green. There are some of each color. How many of each color could there be?* The task is to figure out all the possible combinations.

Comparing Stories

Comparing Stories are the most difficult types of stories to tell. There are three types of comparison stories. The first type of comparison story is where two different things are being compared. For example, *Susie has ten lollipops and Kayla has eight. How many more lollipops does Susie have than Kayla?*

The second type of comparison story is where the bigger part is unknown. In this type of story, we are looking for the bigger amount. For example, *Susie had 4 candies. Maya had 3 more than her. How many candies did Maya have?* Here, we know what Susie had, and then in comparison, Maya had 3 more. The task is to find the bigger part.

The third type of comparison story is to find the smaller part. This is the hardest type of story to tell. For example, *Jaya has 7 candies. She has 3 more than Marcos. How many does Marcos have?* In this type of story we know what Jaya has and we know that she has 3 more than Marcos. We are looking for the smaller amount. We only know about what Marcos has in comparison to what Jaya has. The task is to use the information given to solve for the smaller part.

Two Step Problems

In second grade, students start to do two-step problems where they combine the problem types. For example: *Sue had 5 more marbles than David. David had 4 marbles. How many marbles do they have altogether?* To solve two-step problems, students should have a good understanding of the original problem types and then these are combined into a more complex problem.

The 2ⁿᵈ Grade Word Problem Standards

There are several great tools to use for solving number stories. The CCSS outlines very specific problems that students are supposed to solve. Here are the specific 2nd grade standards that inform the problems in this book. They all come from the CCSSM (2010).

2OA1: Use addition and subtraction within 100 to solve one- and two-step word problems involving situations of adding to, taking from, putting together, taking apart, and comparing, with unknowns in all positions, e.g., by using drawings and equations with a symbol for the unknown number to represent the problem.

2OA6: Add up to four two-digit numbers using strategies based on place value and properties of operations.

2OA4: Compare two three-digit numbers based on meanings of the hundreds, tens, and ones digits, using >, =, and < symbols to record the results of comparisons.

2MD5: Use addition and subtraction within 100 to solve word problems involving lengths that are given in the same units, e.g., by using drawings (such as drawings of rulers) and equations with a symbol for the unknown number to represent the problem.

2MD6: Represent whole numbers as lengths from 0 on a number line diagram with equally spaced points corresponding to the numbers 0, 1, 2, ..., and represent whole-number sums and differences within 100 on a number line diagram.

2MD8: Solve word problems involving dollar bills, quarters, dimes, nickels, and pennies, using $ and ¢symbols appropriately. *Example: If you have 2 dimes and 3 pennies, how many cents do you have?*

2MD9: Generate measurement data by measuring lengths of several objects to the nearest whole unit, or by making repeated measurements of the same object. Show the measurements by making a line plot, where the horizontal scale is marked off in whole-number units.

2MD10: Draw a picture graph and a bar graph (with single-unit scale) to represent a data set with up to four categories. Solve simple put-together, take-apart, and compare problems using information presented in a bar graph.

THE 2ND GRADE MODELS FOR PROBLEM SOLVING

In this book students will use several different tools to model the word problems. They will use Number Frames, the Number Grid, Open Number Line, Drawings, Picture Graphs, Bar Graphs, Line plots and Equations.

Number Frames

Number frames provide a visual scaffold for children to understand word problems. There are 3 different types of number frames: The Five Frame, the ten frame and the double ten frame. Five is the first anchor number so we should always start with Five Frames (in k and 1), although few math programs do. Ten is foundational and many math programs do use this frame. Finally, the double ten frame helps to increase the range of number in word problems. Number frames are visual scaffolds that help students to see what they are doing and think about the numbers in different ways.

TEN FRAME

DOUBLE TEN FRAME

The Number Grid

The number grid is an excellent tool to help students think about counting strategies. On the number grid to do add to result unknown problems, students choose a number to start with and then count on. In terms of efficiency you want to teach students to start with the highest number and count on. You also want to teach them how to break apart numbers and use this method to add efficiently. For example, if the student has the numbers 45 plus 37 you want the student to know to count down 3 tens and then over 7.

1	2	3	4	5	6	7	8	9	10
11	12	13	14	15	16	17	18	19	20
21	22	23	24	25	26	27	28	29	30
31	32	33	34	35	36	37	38	39	40
41	42	43	44	45	46	47	48	49	50
51	52	53	54	55	56	57	58	59	60
61	62	63	64	65	66	67	68	69	70
71	72	73	74	75	76	77	78	79	80
81	82	83	84	85	86	87	88	89	90
91	92	93	94	95	96	97	98	99	100

The Open Number Line

The Open Number Line is an excellent model for students to use. They draw a line, plot numbers on it and count using a variety of strategies. For example, let's take the problem 45 plus 37.

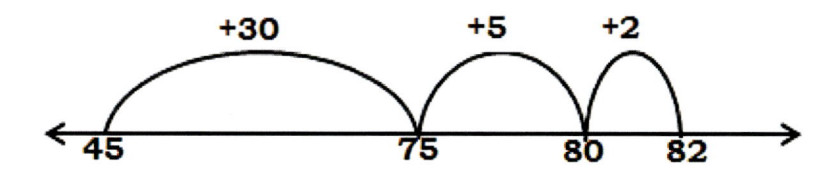

```
        +30        +5    +2
       ⌒         ⌒    ⌒
←——45—————————75——80——82——→
```

The student starts at 45 and jumps 30 because they broke apart the 37 into 30 and 5 and 2. From 75 they jump five more to 80 and then 2 more to 82. Number lines are a huge part of the new math CCSS and it is very important to make sure that students are very comfortable with using them. Students will use number lines throughout the different grades.

Line Plots

Second grade students are expected to use data to make a line plot and then be able to answer questions about the line plot. See the following example:

The 2nd grade made a frequency table of pets per person in their class. Use the data in the frequency table to make a line plot.

Pets Per Person	
Zero Pets	7
1 Pet	5
2 Pets	6
3 Pets	4
4 Pets	2

Line plot of pets per person in our classroom

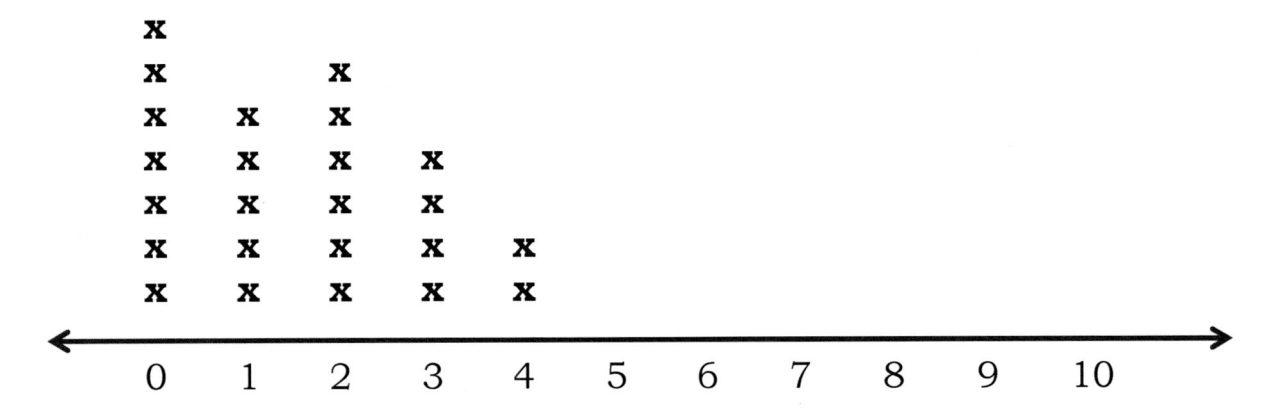

```
x
x
x       x
x   x   x
x   x   x   x
x   x   x   x
x   x   x   x   x
x   x   x   x   x
←――――――――――――――――――――――――→
0   1   2   3   4   5   6   7   8   9   10
```

Line plot Questions:
1. How many people voted altogether?
2. How many more people have no pets than have 2 pets?
3. How many fewer people have 4 pets than have 1 pet?

Money Problems

Students are expected to be able to solve word problems about money with $ and ¢. They can do this with either a number line or drawings of the money. *For example: Sue had 1 quarter and 2 dimes. How much money did she have altogether?*

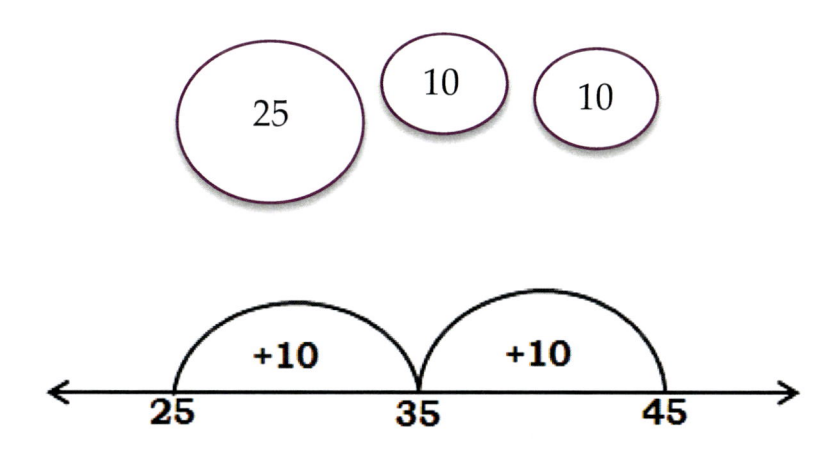

Drawing of a Ruler

The CCSSM actually states that second graders should know how to illustrate their mathematical thinking about measurement through drawings (including rulers). This is very interesting, given that this is not a part of most curriculums. Therefore we have included problems throughout the various sections where students are expected to do this.

Bar Graphs

Second grade students are expected to use data to make a bar graph and then be able to answer questions framed around the different problem types. See the following example:

The 2nd grade voted on their Favorite Animals.
Use the data in the frequency table to make a bar graph.

Favorite Animals	
Birds	20
Cats	40
Dogs	50
Reptiles	30
Other	25

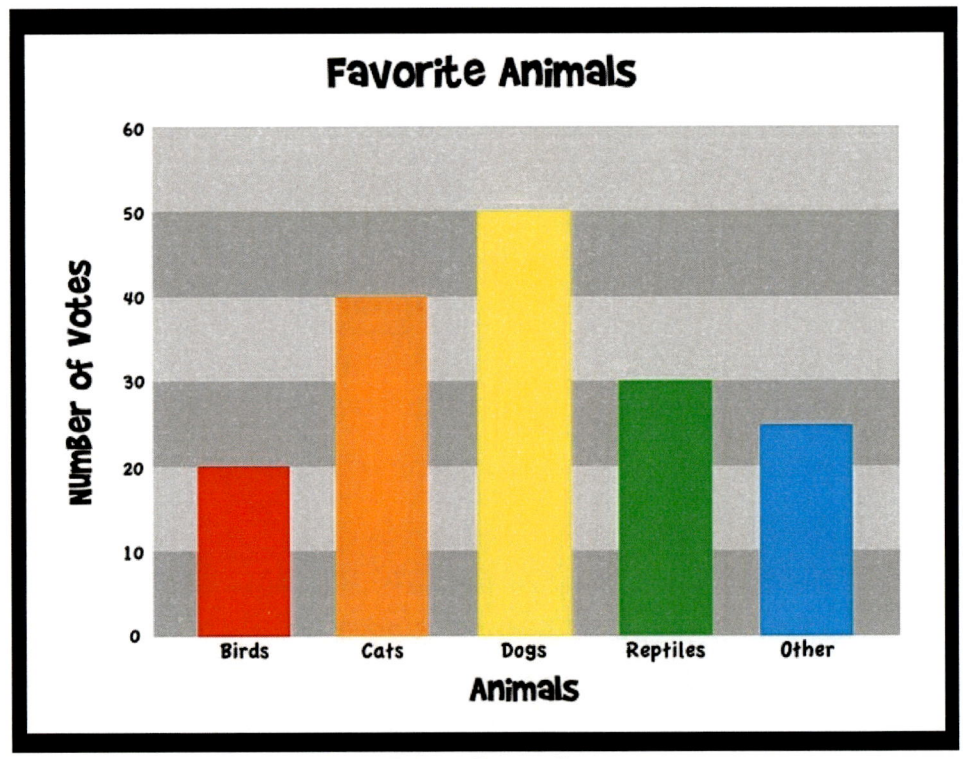

Bar Graph

Questions:
1. How many people voted altogether?
2. How many more people liked cats?
3. How many fewer people liked birds than dogs?

Picture Graph

2nd grade students are expected to use data to make a picture graph and then be able to answer questions about it.

See the following example:

The 2nd grade voted on their favorite animals. Use the data in the frequency table to make a picture graph.

Favorite Animals	
Birds	20
Cats	40
Dogs	50
Reptiles	30
Other	25

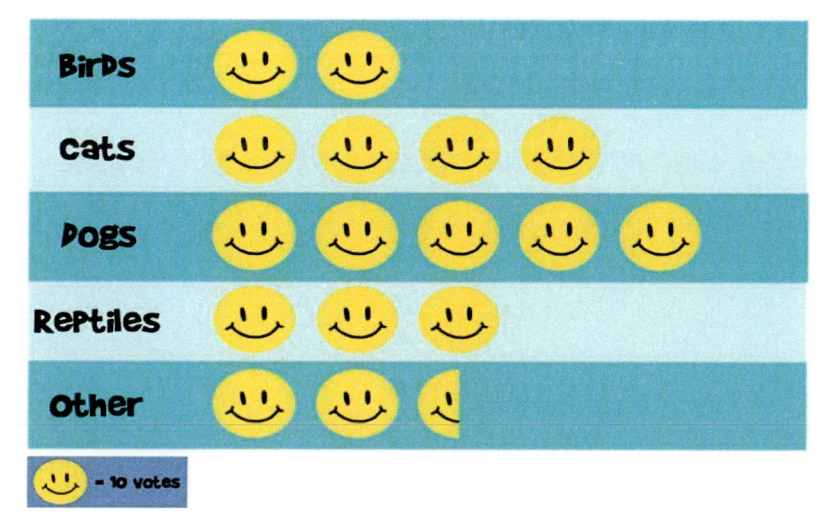

Favorite Animals

Birds: 😊 😊
Cats: 😊 😊 😊 😊
Dogs: 😊 😊 😊 😊 😊
Reptiles: 😊 😊 😊
Other: 😊 😊 ◐

😊 = 10 votes

Picture Graph

Questions:
1. How many people voted altogether?
2. How many more people liked birds?
3. How many fewer people liked reptiles than liked dogs?

Equations

Second Graders are expected to be able to write an equation with a symbol for the unknown. They are also expected to compare numbers using symbols for greater than, less than and equal to. For example: *Sue had 15 cm of string. She bought 27 cm more. How much does she have now?*

$$15 + 27 = ?$$

Another example: *Sue has 57 cm of string. Tara has 34 cm of string. Who has more and how much more?*

$$57 > 34$$

USE BAR/TAPE DIAGRAM

In the CCSSM students are required to know how to use a tape diagram to model their thinking. *Bar diagrams help students to "unpack" the structure of a problem and lay the foundation for its solution" (Diezmann and English, 2001, p. 77 cited in Charles, Monograph 24324). Nickerson (1994) found that the ability to use diagrams is integral to mathematics thinking and learning (cited in Charles).*

In the charts below, I have provided a detailed explanation for each of the CCSS 1-step word problem types for addition and subtraction. The word problem type is designated with a sample problem. Then there is a bar diagram to show the relationships between the quantities. Then there is an explanation of the problem type and the various strategies that can be used to solve the problem. There is also the algebraic equation showing the different operations that can be used to solve the problem. As Charles (Monograph 24324) points out, *"It is important to recognize that a relationship in some word problems can be translated into more than one appropriate number sentence."*

Problem Types	Result Unknown	Change Unknown	Start Unknown
Join/Adding to	Marco had 5 marbles. His brother gave him 5 more. How many does he have now?	Marco had 5 marbles. His brother gave him some more. Now he has 10. How many did his brother give him?	Marco had some marbles. His brother gave him 5 more. Now he has 10. How many did he have in the beginning?
Bar Diagram Modeling Problem	? over [5][5]	10 over [5][?]	10 over [?][5]
What are we looking for? Where is X?	Both addends are known. We are looking for the total amount. The result is the unknown. In other words, we know what we started with and we know the change, we are looking for the end.	The first addend is known. The result is also known. We are looking for the change. The change is unknown. In other words, we know what happened at the start and we know what happened at the end. We are looking for the change. We need to find out what happened in the middle.	The second addend is known. The result is known. We are looking for the start. The start is unknown. In other words, we know the change and we know the end but we don't know what happened at the beginning.
Algebraic Sentence	5 + 5 = ?	5 + ?= 10 10-5=?	x + 5 = 10
Strategies to Solve	Add/ Know number Bonds/Know derived Facts/Count Up	Count Up/Know Bonds/	Count up/Subtract
Answer	5 + 5 = 10 He had ten marbles.	5 + 5 = 10 10 - 5 = 5 He brother gave him five marbles.	5 + 5 = 10 10 - 5 = 5 He had five marbles.

Problem Solving with Math Models© 2012

Problem Types	Result Unknown	Change Unknown	Start Unknown
Separate/ Taking From	Marco had 10 marbles. He gave his brother 4. How many does he have left?	Marco had 10 marbles. He gave some away. Now he has 5 left. How many did he give away?	Marco had some marbles. He gave 2 away and now he has 5 left. How many did he have to start with?
Bar Diagram Modeling Problem	10 / [4 | ?]	10 / [? | 5]	? / [2 | 5]
What are we looking for? Where is X?	In this story we know the beginning and what happened in the middle. The mystery is what happened at the end. The result is unknown.	In this story we know the beginning and the end. The mystery is what happened in the middle. The change is unknown.	In this story we know what happened in the middle and what happened at the end. The mystery is how did it start. The start is unknown.
Algebraic Sentence	10 - 4 =?	10 – ? = 5 5 + x =10	? - 2 = 5 2 + 5 =?
Strategies to Solve	Subtract/ /Use number Bonds Facts/ Know derived Facts (Doubles -1, Doubles -2)	Subtract until you have the result left/ Count Up/Use number Bonds/Use derived facts	Count up/Subtract
Answer	10-4 = 6 He had 6 marbles left.	10-5=5 5 + 5 = 10 He gave away 5 marbles.	7-2=5 2+5=7 He had 7 marbles in the beginning.

Problem Solving with Math Models© 2012

Problem Types	Quantity Unknown	Part Unknown	Both Addends Unknown
Part/Part Whole/Putting together/Taking Apart	Marco has 5 red marbles and 5 blue ones. How many marbles does Marco have? 5 + 5 = x	Marco has 10 marbles. Five are red and the rest are blue. How many are blue? 10 -5 = or 5 + x = 10	Marco has 10 marbles. Some are red and some are blue. How many could be red and how many could be blue?
Bar Diagram Modeling Problem	? ⟷ | 5 | 5 |	10 ⟷ | 5 | ? |	10 ⟷ | ? | ? |
What are we looking for? Where is X?	In this type of story we are talking about a group, set or collection of something. Here we know both parts and we are looking for the total.	In this type of story we are talking about a group, set or collection of something. Here we know the total and one of the parts. We are looking for the amount of the other part.	In this type of story we are talking about a group, set or collection of something. Here we know the total but we are to think about all the possible ways to make the group, set or collection.
Algebraic Sentence	5 + 5 = ?	5 + ? = 10 10-5=?	x + y = 10
Strategies to Solve	Add/ Know number Bonds/Know derived Facts/Count Up	Count Up/Know Bonds/	Count up/Subtract
Answer	5+5=10 He had ten marbles.	5+5=10 10-5 =? Five were blue	1+9 4+6 9+1 6+4 2+8 5+5 8 + 2 3+7 10+0 0 +10 7+3 These are the possibilities

Problem Solving with Math Models© 2012

Problem Types	Difference Unknown	Bigger Part Unknown	Smaller Part Unknown
Compare	Marco has 5 marbles. His brother has 7. How many more marbles does his brother have than he does?	Marco has 5 marbles. His brother has 2 more than he does. How many marbles does his brother have?	Tom has 5 rocks. Marco has 2 less than Tom. How many rocks does Marco have?
Bar Diagram Modeling Problem	[5] ↔? [7]	[5] / [5][2] ?	[5] / [?]
What are we looking for? Where is X?	In this type of story we are comparing two amounts. We are looking for the difference between the two numbers.	In this type of story we are comparing two amounts. We are looking for the bigger part which is unknown.	In this type of story we are comparing two amounts. We are looking for the smaller part which is unknown.
Algebraic Sentence	7-5 =?	5 + ? = 7	5-2=?
Strategies to Solve	Count up/ Count back	Count up	Subtract
Answer	His brother had 2 more marbles than he did.	His brother had 7 marbles.	Marco had 3 marbles.

Teacher Tips:

- When you introduce the problem, be sure to tell the students what type of problem it is.

- Remember that you can take the same problem and rework it in different ways throughout the week.

- Work on a problem type until the students are proficient at recognizing and solving that problem type. Also give them opportunities to write and tell that specific problem type.

- Be sure to contextualize the problems in the students' everyday lives. Using the problems in the book as models, substitute the students' names and their everyday things.

- Be sure to provide tons of guided practice. Solve problems together as a class, with partners and in groups. Individual practice should come after the students have had plenty of opportunities to work together and comprehend and understand what they are doing.

- Emphasize that there is no one correct way to solve a problem but that there is usually only one correct answer.

- Encourage students to always show their work.

UNIT 1 - Add To Problems

CHAPTER 1
ADD TO RESULT UNKNOWN PROBLEMS

These types of problems are the easiest types of addition problems. In these problems students are looking for what happened at the end of the story. We know what we started with and what we added to that part. We are trying to find out how many we have altogether now.

PROBLEM	John had 10 marbles. Henry gave him 7 more. How many does he have now?
MODEL	*number line showing 10 with +7 arc to 17*
EQUATION	10 + 7 = ? 10 + 7 = 17

Unit 1 – Add to Problems

ADD TO RESULT UNKNOWN

1. Lindsay had 2 marbles. Dennis gave her 8 more. How many marbles does Lindsay have now?

Way #1: Solve with a ten frame

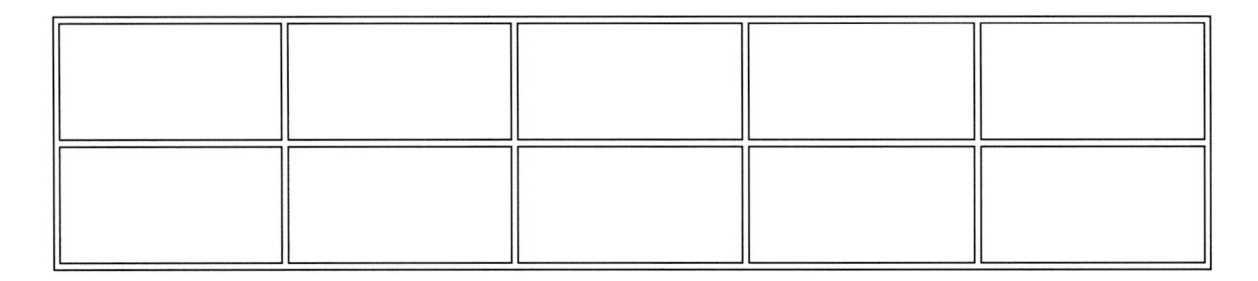

Way #2: Write an equation and use a symbol for the unknown amount. Solve.

Explain your thinking:

Unit 1 – Add to Problems

ADD TO RESULT UNKNOWN

2. Brian had 7 markers. Pat gave him 8 more. How many markers does Brian have now?

Way #1: Solve with a double ten frame

Way #2: Write an equation and use a symbol for the unknown amount. Solve.

Explain your thinking:

Problem Solving with Math Models© 2012

Unit 1 – Add to Problems

ADD TO RESULT UNKNOWN

3. Lauren had 74 flower stamps. Andrew gave her 15 more. How many stamps does Lauren have now?

Way #1: Solve with a number grid

1	2	3	4	5	6	7	8	9	10
11	12	13	14	15	16	17	18	19	20
21	22	23	24	25	26	27	28	29	30
31	32	33	34	35	36	37	38	39	40
41	42	43	44	45	46	47	48	49	50
51	52	53	54	55	56	57	58	59	60
61	62	63	64	65	66	67	68	69	70
71	72	73	74	75	76	77	78	79	80
81	82	83	84	85	86	87	88	89	90
91	92	93	94	95	96	97	98	99	100

Way #2: Write an equation and use a symbol for the unknown amount. Solve.

Explain your thinking:

Unit 1 – Add to Problems

ADD TO RESULT UNKNOWN

4. The class took a vote on their favorite ice creams. Use the data in the frequency table to make a line plot.

Favorite Ice Cream Flavors	
Vanilla	7
Chocolate	10
Strawberry	4
Other	9

Draw a line plot to represent the data

Question 1: How many people voted altogether?

Question 2: How many people liked vanilla and chocolate together?

Question 3: Write a question about this data

Problem Solving with Math Models© 2012

Unit 1 – Add to Problems

ADD TO RESULT UNKNOWN

5. The class took a vote on their favorite sea animals. Use the data in the frequency table to make a picture graph.

Favorite Sea Animals	
Whales	9
Sharks	11
Squid/Octopus	4
Other	5

Draw a picture graph to represent the data

Question 1: How many people voted altogether?

Question 2: How many people liked whales and sharks altogether?

Question 3: Write a question about this data

Unit 1 – Add to Problems

ADD TO RESULT UNKNOWN

6. Joe had 53 pennies. Omar gave him 2 dimes. How much money does Joe have now?

Way #1: Solve with a bar diagram or drawings

Way #2: Write an equation and use a symbol for the unknown amount. Solve.

Explain your thinking:

Unit 1 – Add to Problems

ADD TO RESULT UNKNOWN

7. Jenna cut 45 cm of string to make bracelets. Then she cut 17 more cm of string. How many cm of string did she cut altogether?

Way #1: Solve with an open number line

Way #2: Write an equation and use a symbol for the unknown amount. Solve.

Explain your thinking:

ADD TO RESULT UNKNOWN

8. The class voted on their favorite pets. Use the data in the frequency table to make a bar graph:

Favorite Pets	
Dogs	10
Cats	5
Fish	9
Reptiles	5

Draw a bar graph to represent the data

Question 1: How many people voted altogether?

Question 2: How many people liked dogs and cats together?

Question 3: Write a question about this data

Unit 1 – Add to Problems

CHAPTER 1 QUIZ:
ADD TO RESULT UNKNOWN

Solve with a model:

1. Francisco had 7 marbles. His brother gave him 10 more. How many does he have now?

2. Marta had 15 rings. She got 8 more for her birthday. How many rings does she have now?

3. David had 8 action figures. He bought 4 more. How many does he have now?

Unit 1 – Add to Problems

4. The class voted on their favorite zoo animal. Use the data in the frequency table to Make a line plot:

Favorite Zoo Animals	
Amphibians	7
Mammals	12
Birds	4
Reptiles	5

Draw a line plot to represent the data

Question 1: How many people voted altogether?

Question 2: How many people liked mammals and birds altogether?

Question 3: Write a question about this data.

Unit 1 – Add to Problems

CHAPTER 2
ADD TO CHANGE UNKNOWN PROBLEMS

In these problems students are looking for what happened in the middle of the story. In this type of story we know what happened at the beginning but then some change happened and now we have more than we started with at the end. We are trying to find out how many things were added in the middle of the story.

PROBLEM	John had 5 baseballs. His mother gave him some more. Now he has 12. How many did his mother give him?
MODEL	+7 arc from 5 to 12 on a number line
EQUATION	5 + ? = 12 5 + 7 = 12

Unit 1 – Add to Problems

ADD TO CHANGE UNKNOWN

1. Chandler had 6 toy airplanes. Mitt gave him some more airplanes. Now he has 10 airplanes. How many airplanes did Mitt give him?

Way #1: Solve with a ten frame

Way #2: Write an equation and use a symbol for the unknown amount. Solve.

Explain your thinking:

Unit 1 – Add to Problems

ADD TO CHANGE UNKNOWN

2. Jill had 10 cookies. Jane gave her some more cookies. Jill has 20 cookies now. How many cookies did Jane give her?

Way #1: Solve with a double ten frame

Way #2: Write an equation and use a symbol for the unknown amount. Solve.

Explain your thinking:

Unit 1 – Add to Problems

ADD TO CHANGE UNKNOWN

3. Jacqueline had 8 inches of string. She bought some more inches of string. Now she has 12 inches of string. How much did she buy?

Way #1: Solve with a drawing of a ruler

Way #2: Write an equation and use a symbol for the unknown amount. Solve.

Explain your thinking:

Unit 1 – Add to Problems

ADD TO CHANGE UNKNOWN

4. Deon had 25 toy cars. Stephen gave him some more toy cars. Deon has 36 toy cars now. How many toy cars did Stephen give to Deon?

Way #1: Solve with a number grid

1	2	3	4	5	6	7	8	9	10
11	12	13	14	15	16	17	18	19	20
21	22	23	24	25	26	27	28	29	30
31	32	33	34	35	36	37	38	39	40
41	42	43	44	45	46	47	48	49	50
51	52	53	54	55	56	57	58	59	60
61	62	63	64	65	66	67	68	69	70
71	72	73	74	75	76	77	78	79	80
81	82	83	84	85	86	87	88	89	90
91	92	93	94	95	96	97	98	99	100

Way #2: Write an equation and use a symbol for the unknown amount. Solve.

Explain your thinking:

Unit 1 – Add to Problems

ADD TO CHANGE UNKNOWN

5. Clare had 56 cents. For her birthday she received some more. Now she has 72 cents. How much money did she get for her birthday?

Way #1: Solve with an bar diagram

Way #2: Write an equation and use a symbol for the unknown amount. Solve.

Explain your thinking:

Unit 1 – Add to Problems

ADD TO CHANGE UNKNOWN

6. The class voted on their favorite colors. Use the data in the frequency table to make a line plot:

Favorite Colors	
Purple	4
Pink	11
Orange	8
Other	7

Draw a line plot to represent the data

Question 1: How many people voted altogether?

Question 2: How many people more people would have to like purple to be equal to the people who like pink?

Question 3: Write a question about this graph

Problem Solving with Math Models© 2012

ADD TO CHANGE UNKNOWN

7. There were 7 dimes in the piggy bank. Dad put some more dimes in the jar and now there is 90 cents. How much money did he put in the piggy bank?

Way #1: Solve with an open number line or a drawing

Way #2: Write an equation and use a symbol for the unknown amount. Solve.

Explain your thinking:

Unit 1 – Add to Problems

ADD TO CHANGE UNKNOWN

8. The class voted on their favorite types of TV shows. Use the data in the frequency table to make a picture graph.

Favorite TV Shows	
Cartoons	14
Reality Shows	3
Cop Shows	2
Comedies	7

Draw a picture graph to represent the data

Question 1: How many people voted altogether?

Question 2: How many more people would have to like comedies to be equal to the amount of people that like cartoons?

Question 3: Write a question about this graph.

Unit 1 – Add to Problems

CHAPTER 2 QUIZ: ADD TO CHANGE UNKNOWN PROBLEMS

Solve with a model:

1. Sue had 5 stickers and John gave her some more. Now she has 10 stickers. How many did John give her?

2. Carlos had 5 pennies and 3 dimes. His mother gave him some more money. Now he has 50 cents. How much more money did his mother give him?

Problem Solving with Math Models© 2012

Unit 1 – Add to Problems

3. The bakery baked 27 cupcakes in the morning. In the afternoon they baked 10 more. In the evening they baked even more and now they have 58 cupcakes. How many more did they bake in the evening?

4. Melissa bought 3 inches of string. Then she bought 5 inches more. How much string did she buy altogether?

Unit 1 – Add to Problems

CHAPTER 3
ADD TO START UNKNOWN PROBLEMS

In these problems students are looking for what happened in the beginning of the story. In this type of story we know what happened in the middle and we know how many we ended up with but we are looking for how the story started.

PROBLEM	John had some marbles. Henry gave him 7 more. Now he has 14. How many did he have in the beginning?
MODEL	A number line showing a jump of +7 from 7 to 14.
EQUATION	? + 7 = 14 7 + 7 = 14

Unit 1 – Add to Problems

ADD TO START UNKNOWN

1. Danielle had some gummy bears. Samantha gave her 5 more. Now she has 10 gummy bears. How many gummy bears did she have in the beginning?

Way #1: Solve with a ten frame

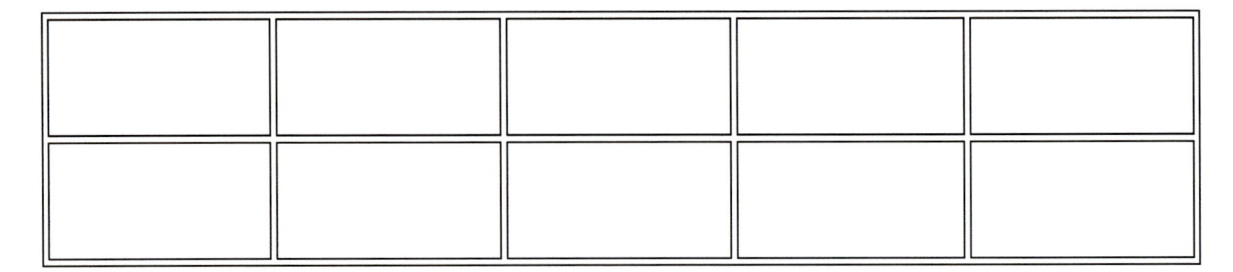

Way #2: Write an equation and use a symbol for the unknown amount. Solve.

Explain your thinking:

Unit 1 – Add to Problems

ADD TO START UNKNOWN

2. Ethan had some building blocks. Charlie gave him 5 more. Now he has 14 blocks. How many blocks did he have in the beginning?

Way#1: Solve with a double ten frame

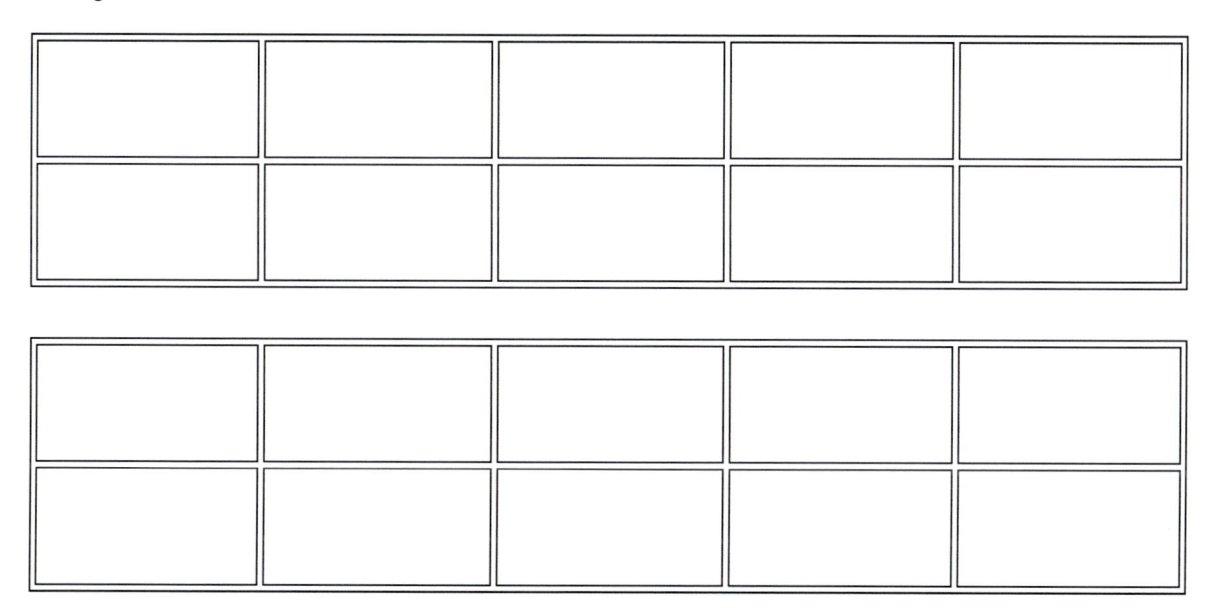

Way#2: Write an equation and use a symbol for the unknown amount. Solve.

Explain your thinking:

Unit 1 – Add to Problems

ADD TO START UNKNOWN

3. The bakery had some cookies. They baked 24 more strawberry ones. Now, they have 100. How many cookies did they have in the beginning?

Way #1: Solve with an open number line

Way #2: Write an equation and use a symbol for the unknown amount. Solve.

Explain your thinking:

Unit 1 – Add to Problems

ADD TO START UNKNOWN

4. The candy store had some lollipops. They got a shipment of 40 and now they have 89. How many did they have in the beginning?

Way #1: Solve with a number grid

1	2	3	4	5	6	7	8	9	10
11	12	13	14	15	16	17	18	19	20
21	22	23	24	25	26	27	28	29	30
31	32	33	34	35	36	37	38	39	40
41	42	43	44	45	46	47	48	49	50
51	52	53	54	55	56	57	58	59	60
61	62	63	64	65	66	67	68	69	70
71	72	73	74	75	76	77	78	79	80
81	82	83	84	85	86	87	88	89	90
91	92	93	94	95	96	97	98	99	100

Way #2: Write an equation and use a symbol for the unknown amount. Solve.

Explain your thinking:

Problem Solving with Math Models© 2012

Unit 1 – Add to Problems

ADD TO START UNKNOWN

5. The school store had some pencils. They got a shipment of 38 blue ones, 22 green ones and 15 orange ones. Now they have 100 pencils. How many did they have in the beginning?

Way #1: Solve with a bar diagram

Way #2: Write an equation and use a symbol for the unknown amount. Solve.

Explain your thinking:

Unit 1 – Add to Problems

ADD TO START UNKNOWN

6. Jason had some money. He got 3 nickels, 4 dimes and 3 pennies for his birthday. Now, he has 63 cents. How much did he have in the beginning?

Way #1: Solve with a number grid

1	2	3	4	5	6	7	8	9	10
11	12	13	14	15	16	17	18	19	20
21	22	23	24	25	26	27	28	29	30
31	32	33	34	35	36	37	38	39	40
41	42	43	44	45	46	47	48	49	50
51	52	53	54	55	56	57	58	59	60
61	62	63	64	65	66	67	68	69	70
71	72	73	74	75	76	77	78	79	80
81	82	83	84	85	86	87	88	89	90
91	92	93	94	95	96	97	98	99	100

Way #2: Write an equation and use a symbol for the unknown amount. Solve.

Explain your thinking:

Problem Solving with Math Models© 2012

Unit 1 – Add to Problems

ADD TO START UNKNOWN

7. Mandy cut some string. Then she cut 9 more inches. Altogether she cut 11 inches of string. How much did she cut in the beginning?

Way #1: Solve with a drawing of a ruler

Way #2: Write an equation and use a symbol for the unknown amount. Solve.

Explain your thinking:

Unit 1 – Add to Problems

ADD TO START UNKNOWN

8. The circus had some stuffed animals. They got a shipment of 34 bears and 22 lions and now they have 84 stuffed animals. How many did they have in the beginning?

Way#1: Solve with an open number line

Way#2: Write an equation and use a symbol for the unknown amount. Solve.

Explain your thinking:

Unit 1 – Add to Problems

CHAPTER 3 QUIZ: ADD TO START UNKNOWN PROBLEMS

Solve with a model:

1. Kelly had some bracelets. She got 7 more for her birthday. Now she has 14. How many did she have in the beginning?

2. Kent bought some steaks. Then he bought 12 more steaks. Now, he has 24 steaks. How much did he have in the beginning?

Unit 1 – Add to Problems

3. Marcus had some money. His brother gave him 4 nickels and a quarter. Now he has 70 cents. How much money did he have in the beginning?

4. The pizza shop made pizzas in the morning. In the afternoon they made 55 more. Now they have 71 pizzas. How many did they make in the morning?

Unit 1 – Add to Problems

UNIT 1 TEST:
ADDITION PROBLEMS

Solve with a model:

1. Kim had 25 dollhouses. For her birthday she got 59 more. How many dollhouses does she have altogether now?

2. Raul had 25 cents. His sister gave him a quarter and 2 dimes. How much money does he have now?

Unit 1 – Add to Problems

3. The bakery made 48 cakes in the morning and some more cakes in the afternoon. Now they have 100 cakes. How many did they make in the afternoon?

4. David had some baseball trading cards. He got 20 more. Now he has 50. How many did he have in the beginning?

UNIT 2 - Take From Problems

CHAPTER 1
TAKE FROM RESULT UNKNOWN PROBLEMS

In these problems students are looking for what happened in the end of the story. In this type of story we know what happened at the beginning and also what change occurred. We are trying to find out how many things remained after some things were taken away.

PROBLEM	John had 10 apples. He gave 5 away. How many does he have left?
MODEL	(number line showing arc labeled -5 from 10 back to 5)
EQUATION	10 – ? = 5

Problem Solving with Math Models© 2012

Unit 2 – Take From Problems

TAKE FROM RESULT UNKNOWN

1. Mrs. Smith picked 10 apples from the apple tree. She ate 3 apples and gave 4 apples to her daughter. How many apples does she have left?

Way #1: Solve with a ten frame

Way #2: Write an equation and use a symbol for the unknown amount. Solve.

Explain your thinking:

Unit 2 – Take From Problems

TAKE FROM RESULT UNKNOWN

2. Cameron had 17 crayons. He gave 4 to Heather and 4 to John. How many crayons does he have left?

Way #1: Solve with a double ten frame

Way #2: Write an equation and use a symbol for the unknown amount. Solve.

Explain your thinking:

TAKE FROM RESULT UNKNOWN

3. Brian had $.50. He gave his brother a quarter and his sister a dime. How much money does he have left?

Way #1: Solve with an open number line or drawings

Way #2: Write an equation and use a symbol for the unknown amount. Solve.

Explain your thinking:

Unit 2 – Take From Problems

TAKE FROM RESULT UNKNOWN

4. Tamera had 100 butterfly stamps. She used 28 stamps. How many stamps does she have left?

Way #1: Solve with a number grid

1	2	3	4	5	6	7	8	9	10
11	12	13	14	15	16	17	18	19	20
21	22	23	24	25	26	27	28	29	30
31	32	33	34	35	36	37	38	39	40
41	42	43	44	45	46	47	48	49	50
51	52	53	54	55	56	57	58	59	60
61	62	63	64	65	66	67	68	69	70
71	72	73	74	75	76	77	78	79	80
81	82	83	84	85	86	87	88	89	90
91	92	93	94	95	96	97	98	99	100

Way #2: Write an equation and use a symbol for the unknown amount. Solve.

Explain your thinking:

Unit 2 – Take From Problems

TAKE FROM RESULT UNKNOWN

5. Benjamin had 12 inches of wood. He cut 5 inches of it. How much does he have left?

Way #1: Model with a drawing of a ruler

Way #2: Write an equation and use a symbol for the unknown amount. Solve.

Explain your thinking:

Unit 2 – Take From Problems

TAKE FROM RESULT UNKNOWN

6. Blaire had 96 stickers. She gave 27 stickers to her sister. How many stickers does she have left?

Way #1: Solve with an open number line

Way #2: Write an equation and use a symbol for the unknown amount. Solve.

Explain your thinking:

Take From Result Unknown

7. Farmer Serena had 100 lemon trees. She sold 59 of them to the store. How many trees does she have left?

Way #1: Solve with a bar diagram

Way #2: Write an equation and use a symbol for the unknown amount. Solve.

Explain your thinking:

Unit 2 – Take From Problems

TAKE FROM RESULT UNKNOWN

8. Judy had 36 inches of string. She cut 19 inches of it to make some jewelry. How much string does she have left?

Way #1: Solve with an open number line

Way #2: Write an equation and use a symbol for the unknown amount. Solve.

Explain your thinking:

Unit 2 – Take From Problems

CHAPTER 1 QUIZ: TAKE FROM RESULT UNKNOWN PROBLEMS

Solve with a model:

1. Mark had 92 cents. He gave away a quarter, a nickel and a dime. How much money does he have left?

2. Mary had 100 seashells. She gave 37 of them away. How many does she have left now?

Unit 2 – Take From Problems

3. Daniel had 11 inches of rope. He cut 9 inches of it. How much rope did he have left?

4. The jewelry store had 88 rings. They sold 59 of them. How many do they have left now?

Unit 2 – Take From Problems

CHAPTER 2
TAKE FROM CHANGE UNKNOWN PROBLEMS

In these problems students are looking for what happened in the middle of the story. In this type of story we know what happened at the beginning but then some change happened and now we have less than we started with by the end of the story. We are trying to find out how many things were taken away in the middle of the story.

PROBLEM	John had 15 marbles. He gave some to his cousin. Now he has 12 left. How many did he give to his cousin?
MODEL	*number line showing jumps from 15 back to 12, labeled - 3*
EQUATION	15 – ? = 12

Unit 2 – Take From Problems

TAKE FROM CHANGE UNKNOWN

1. Patrice had 10 strawberries. She gave Erin some strawberries. Now she has 5 strawberries left. How many strawberries did Patrice give Erin?

Way #1: Solve with a ten frame

Way #2: Write an equation and use a symbol for the unknown amount. Solve.

Explain your thinking:

Unit 2 – Take From Problems

TAKE FROM CHANGE UNKNOWN

2. Denise had 17 grapes. She ate some grapes. Now she has 10 grapes left. How many grapes did she eat?

Way #1: Solve with a double ten frame

Way #2: Write an equation and use a symbol for the unknown amount. Solve.

Explain your thinking:

Unit 2 – Take From Problems

TAKE FROM CHANGE UNKNOWN

3. The bakery had 100 chocolate bars. They sold some and now they have 20 left. How many chocolate bars did they sell?

Way #1: Solve with an open number line

Way #2: Write an equation and use a symbol for the unknown amount. Solve.

Explain your thinking:

Unit 2 – Take From Problems

TAKE FROM CHANGE UNKNOWN

4. The candy store had 79 packs of gum. They sold some and now they have 23 left. How many did they sell?

Way#1: Solve with a number grid

1	2	3	4	5	6	7	8	9	10
11	12	13	14	15	16	17	18	19	20
21	22	23	24	25	26	27	28	29	30
31	32	33	34	35	36	37	38	39	40
41	42	43	44	45	46	47	48	49	50
51	52	53	54	55	56	57	58	59	60
61	62	63	64	65	66	67	68	69	70
71	72	73	74	75	76	77	78	79	80
81	82	83	84	85	86	87	88	89	90
91	92	93	94	95	96	97	98	99	100

Way#2: Write an equation and use a symbol for the unknown amount. Solve.

Explain your thinking:

Problem Solving with Math Models© 2012

Unit 2 – Take From Problems

TAKE FROM CHANGE UNKNOWN

5. Mario had 78 cents. He gave some money away and now he has one quarter left. How much money did he give away?

Way #1: Solve with an open number line or drawings

Way #2: Write an equation and use a symbol for the unknown amount. Solve.

Explain your thinking:

Unit 2 – Take From Problems

TAKE FROM CHANGE UNKNOWN

6. Farmer Maxine had 100 bunnies. She sold some bunnies. Now Farmer Maxine has 15 bunnies left. How many bunnies did Farmer Maxine sell?

Way#1: Solve with a bar diagram

Way#2: Write an equation and use a symbol for the unknown amount. Solve.

Explain your thinking:

Unit 2 – Take From Problems

TAKE FROM CHANGE UNKNOWN

7. Susie had 36 inches of fabric. She cut some. Now she has 7 inches of fabric left. How many inches did she cut?

Way #1: Solve with an open number line

Way #2: Write an equation and use a symbol for the unknown amount. Solve.

Explain your thinking:

Unit 2 – Take From Problems

TAKE FROM CHANGE UNKNOWN

8. The magazine store had 83 magazines. They sold many during the week. Now, they have 4 left. How many did they sell?

Way #1: Solve with a bar diagram

Way #2: Write an equation and use a symbol for the unknown amount. Solve.

Explain your thinking:

Unit 2 – Take From Problems

Chapter 2 Quiz:
Take from Change Unknown Problems

Solve with a model:

1. Luisa had 88 cents. She gave away some of it. She now has a quarter left. How much money did she give away?

2. Mary had 80 seashells. She gave some away. Now she has 44 left. How many seashells did she give away?

Unit 2 – Take From Problems

3. May had 100 cm of string. She cut some of it. Now she has 39 cm left. How much string did she cut?

4. The jewelry store had 100 rings. They sold some of them. Now they have 50 left. How many did they sell?

CHAPTER 3
TAKE FROM START UNKNOWN PROBLEMS

In these problems students are looking for how many things there were at the beginning of the story. In this type of story we only know that there was some amount and that there was a change (some things were taken away). We know what was taken away and how much was left. We are trying to find out how much we had in the beginning of the story.

PROBLEM	John had some marbles. He gave his brother 5. Now he has 10 left. How many did he have in the beginning?
MODEL	
EQUATION	? − 5 = 10 15 − 5 = 10

Unit 2 – Take From Problems

TAKE FROM START UNKNOWN

1. Blair had some pencils. She gave Kimberly 3 pencils. Now she has 6 pencils left. How many pencils did she have in the beginning?

Way #1: Solve with a ten frame

Way #2: Write an equation and use a symbol for the unknown amount. Solve.

Explain your thinking:

Unit 2 – Take From Problems

TAKE FROM START UNKNOWN

2. Sean had some gummy bears. He gave Mickey 8 gummy bears. Now he has 12 gummy bears left. How many gummy bears did he have in the beginning?

Way #1: Solve with a double ten frame

Way #2: Write an equation and use a symbol for the unknown amount. Solve.

Explain your thinking:

Take From Start Unknown

3. The ice cream shop had some waffle cones. They sold 94 and now they have 22 left. How many waffle cones did they have to start?

Way#1: Solve with a bar diagram

Way#2: Write an equation and use a symbol for the unknown amount. Solve.

Explain your thinking:

Unit 2 – Take From Problems

TAKE FROM START UNKNOWN

4. Mari had some string. She cut 44 cm of it. Now she has 20 cm left. How much did she have in the beginning?

Way#1: Solve with an open number line

Way#2: Write an equation and use a symbol for the unknown amount. Solve.. Solve.

Explain your thinking:

Unit 2 – Take From Problems

TAKE FROM START UNKNOWN

5. Luke had some yarn. He cut 7 inches. He has 3 inches left of it. How much did he have in the beginning?

Way #1: Solve with a drawing of a ruler

Way #2: Write an equation and use a symbol for the unknown amount. Solve.

Explain your thinking:

Unit 2 – Take From Problems

TAKE FROM START UNKNOWN

6. The toy store had some action figures. They sold 55 and now they have 25 left. How much did they have in the beginning?

Way #1: Solve with an open number line

Way #2: Write an equation and use a symbol for the unknown amount. Solve.

Explain your thinking:

Unit 2 – Take From Problems

Take From Start Unknown

7. The bakery had some cookies. They sold 27 cookies and now they have 42 left. How many did they have to start?

Way #1: Solve with an open number line

Way #2: Write an equation and use a symbol for the unknown amount. Solve.

Explain your thinking:

Unit 2 – Take From Problems

TAKE FROM START UNKNOWN

8. Sara had some bracelets. She gave 5 to her sister. Now she has 15 left. How many did she have in the beginning?

Way #1: Solve with an open number line

Way #2: Write an equation and use a symbol for the unknown amount. Solve.

Explain your thinking:

Unit 2 – Take From Problems

Chapter 3 Quiz: Take From Start Unknown Problems

Solve with a model:

1. Lucy had some money. She gave away a quarter and now she has 55 cents left. How much money did she have in the beginning?

2. Jamal had some string. He cut 4 inches of it. He now has 7 inches left. How much string did he have in the beginning?

Unit 2 – Take From Problems

3. Grandma baked some brownies. She gave away 36 and now she has 48. How many brownies did she have in the beginning?

4. The car shop had some tires. They sold 50 and now they have 50 left. How many did they have in the beginning?

Problem Solving with Math Models© 2012

Unit 2 Test: Take From Problems

Solve with a model:

1. Mark had 55 marbles. He gave away 23. How many does he have left?

2. Zoe had some rope chain to make necklaces. She cut 88 cm. Now she has 12 cm left. How much rope chain did she have in the beginning?

Unit 2 – Take From Problems

3. Dara had 94 cents. She gave away some money. Now she has 7 dimes left. How much money did she did she give away?

4. Kelly had some stickers. She gave away 25 of them and now she has 50 left. How many did she have in the beginning?

UNIT 3 - Put Together/Take Apart Problems

CHAPTER 1
PUT TOGETHER/TAKE APART PROBLEMS

These types of problems are about sets of things. In them we know both parts and we are looking for the whole. What distinguishes a Put Together/Take Apart Problem from an Add to Result Unknown problem is action. In a Put together/Take Apart Problem there is no action only a set of something.

PROBLEM	John had five red apples and five green ones. How many apples did he have altogether?
MODEL	
EQUATION	5 + 5 = ? 5 + 5 = 10

Unit 3 – Put Together /Take Apart Problems

Put Together/Take Apart - Whole Unknown

1. Thomas has 7 cats and 3 dogs. How many pets does Thomas have?

Way #1: Solve with a ten frame

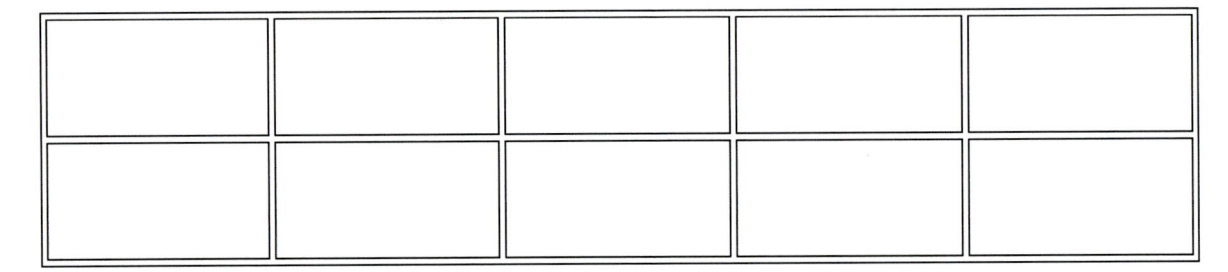

Way #2: Write an equation and use a symbol for the unknown amount. Solve.

Explain your thinking:

Unit 3 – Put Together /Take Apart Problems

PUT TOGETHER/TAKE APART - WHOLE UNKNOWN

2. Natalia has 12 yellow hats and 7 pink hats. How many hats does Natalia have in all?

Way #1: Solve with a double ten frame

Way #2: Write an equation and use a symbol for the unknown amount. Solve.

Explain your thinking:

Unit 3 – Put Together /Take Apart Problems

PUT TOGETHER/TAKE APART - WHOLE UNKNOWN

3. John had 5 nickels, 2 dimes and a quarter. How much money does he have altogether?

Way#1: Solve with a number line or a drawing

Way#2: Write an equation and use a symbol for the unknown amount. Solve.

Explain your thinking:

Unit 3 – Put Together /Take Apart Problems

PUT TOGETHER/TAKE APART - WHOLE UNKNOWN

4. Kate has 35 butterfly stickers and 56 flower stickers. How many stickers does she have altogether?

Way #1: Solve with a number grid

1	2	3	4	5	6	7	8	9	10
11	12	13	14	15	16	17	18	19	20
21	22	23	24	25	26	27	28	29	30
31	32	33	34	35	36	37	38	39	40
41	42	43	44	45	46	47	48	49	50
51	52	53	54	55	56	57	58	59	60
61	62	63	64	65	66	67	68	69	70
71	72	73	74	75	76	77	78	79	80
81	82	83	84	85	86	87	88	89	90
91	92	93	94	95	96	97	98	99	100

Way #2: Write an equation and use a symbol for the unknown amount. Solve.

Explain your thinking:

Problem Solving with Math Models© 2012

Unit 3 – Put Together /Take Apart Problems

PUT TOGETHER/TAKE APART - WHOLE UNKNOWN

5. The class took a vote on their favorite types of books. Use the data in the frequency table to make a line plot.

Favorite Types of Books	
Sports	12
Mysteries	6
Comedies	4
Other	5

Draw a line plot to represent the data

Question 1: How many people voted altogether?

Question 2: How many people liked mysteries and comedies altogether?

Question 3: Write a question about this data

Unit 3 – Put Together /Take Apart Problems

Put Together/Take Apart - Whole Unknown

6. The class took a vote on their favorite flavors of gum. Use the data in the frequency table to make a bar graph.

Favorite Flavors of Gum	
Cherry	5
Rainbow	7
Grape	9
Other	8

Draw a bar graph to represent the data

Question 1: How many people voted altogether?

Question 2: How many people liked grape and cherry altogether?

Question 3: Write a question about this data

Problem Solving with Math Models© 2012

Unit 3 – Put Together /Take Apart Problems

PUT TOGETHER/TAKE APART - WHOLE UNKNOWN

7. The class took a vote on their favorite types of dogs. Use the data in the frequency table to make a picture graph.

Favorite Types of Dogs	
Poodles	3
Labradors	5
Dalmatians	15
Other	8

Draw a picture graph to represent the data

Question 1: How many people voted altogether?

Question 2: How many people liked Labradors and Dalmatians altogether?

Question 3: Write a question about this data

Put Together/Take Apart—Whole Unknown

8. The toy store had 29 footballs, 10 baseballs, 20 tennis balls and 34 soccer balls. How many balls did they have altogether?

Way #1: Solve with a bar diagram

Way #2: Write an equation and use a symbol for the unknown amount. Solve.

Explain your thinking:

Unit 3 – Put Together /Take Apart Problems

Chapter 1 Quiz: Put Together/ Take Apart – Whole Unknown Problems

Solve with a model:

1. Lucy had 5 cm of green string, 3 cm of blue string and 4 cm of pink string. How much string did she have altogether?

2. Marco had 2 quarters, 4 nickels and 2 dimes. How much money did he have altogether?

3. The toy store had 26 footballs and 39 soccer balls. How many balls did they have altogether?

Unit 3 – Put Together /Take Apart Problems

4. The class took a vote on their favorite types of pizza. Use the data in the frequency table to make a line plot.

Favorite Types of Pizza	
Pepperoni	15
Veggie	4
Chicken	7
Other	6

Draw a line plot to represent the data

Question 1: How many people voted altogether?

Question 2: How many people liked pepperoni and chicken altogether?

Question 3: Write a question about this data.

Unit 3 – Put Together /Take Apart Problems

CHAPTER 2
PUT TOGETHER/ TAKE APART– BOTH ADDENDS UNKNOWN

These types of problems are Put Together/Take Apart problems with both addends unknown. In these problems we are talking about sets of something. In this particular type of problem we are talking about all the ways a set can be put together. For example, we have 4 markers. Some are green and some are yellow. How many could be green and how many could be yellow? We could have 3 green and 1 yellow, 2 green and 2 yellow or 1 green and 3 yellow. Students have to find all the ways to do that problem.

With this type of problem we could model our thinking by using real objects, pictures, diagrams, or tables. When you have your students use concrete materials, they can see what is happening. When you have the students solve it with pictures they learn how to organize information and draw it out. Then, when they use a table, they are working at an abstract level.

You want to emphasize that it is important to organize information in a way that other people can tell what you did. We have to show our work. You also want to show students what the equation to match the story looks like.

Unit 3 – Put Together /Take Apart Problems

Way#1: Try drawing pictures to help!

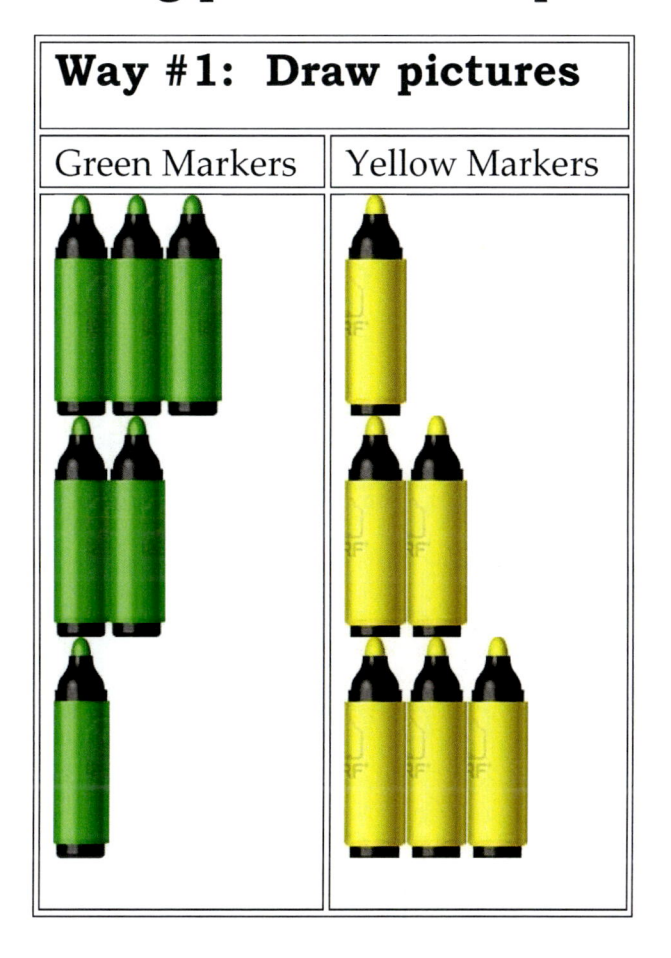

Way #1: Draw pictures	
Green Markers	Yellow Markers

Way#2: Using the Table technique.

MARKERS	
GREEN	*YELLOW*
3	1
2	2
1	3

Problem Solving with Math Models© 2012

Unit 3 – Put Together /Take Apart Problems

PUT TOGETHER/TAKE APART--BOTH ADDENDS UNKNOWN

1. Donna has 8 skirts. Some of the skirts are pink and some of the skirts are green. How many of each type of skirt could she have? She has some of each.

Way#1: Draw pictures

Way#2: Solve with a table (fill in the table)

SKIRTS	
Pink	Green
7	1
6	
5	
4	
3	
2	
1	

Unit 3 – Put Together /Take Apart Problems

PUT TOGETHER/TAKE APART--BOTH ADDENDS UNKNOWN

2. Jennifer has 5 new students in her class. Some of the students are girls and some students are boys. How many students could be girls? How many students could be boys? There are some of each.

Way#1: Draw pictures

Way#2: Solve with a table (fill in the table)

STUDENTS IN CLASS	
Girls	Boys
4	1
3	
2	
1	

Problem Solving with Math Models© 2012

Unit 3 – Put Together /Take Apart Problems

PUT TOGETHER/TAKE APART--BOTH ADDENDS UNKNOWN

3. Sean and Chris ordered 6 slices of pizza. Some of the slices are pepperoni and some of the slices are plain cheese. How many slices could be pepperoni? How many slices could be plain cheese? There are some of each.

Way#1: Draw pictures

Way#2: Solve with a table (fill in the table)

| SLICES OF PIZZA ||
Pepperoni	Cheese
5	
4	
3	
2	
1	

Unit 3 – Put Together /Take Apart Problems

Put Together/Take Apart--Both Addends Unknown

4. There are 4 bears in the zoo. Some of the bears are brown and some of the bears are black. How many bears could be brown? How many bears could be black? There are some of each.

Way#1: Draw pictures

Way#2: Solve with a table (fill in the table)

BEARS IN THE ZOO	
Brown	Black
3	
2	
1	

Problem Solving with Math Models© 2012

Unit 3 – Put Together /Take Apart Problems

PUT TOGETHER/TAKE APART--BOTH ADDENDS UNKNOWN

5. Lydia has 3 cats. Some cats are black and some cats are striped. How many cats could be black? How many cats could be striped? There are some of each.

Way#1: Draw pictures

Way#2: Solve with a table (fill in the table)

CATS	
Black	Striped
2	
1	

Unit 3 – Put Together /Take Apart Problems

PUT TOGETHER/TAKE APART--BOTH ADDENDS UNKNOWN

6. Evan has 5 books. Some books are about airplanes and some books are about cars. How many books could be about airplanes? How many books could be about cars? There are some of each.

Way #1: Draw pictures

Way #2: Solve with a table (fill in the table)

BOOKS	
Books about Planes	Books about Cars
4	
3	
2	
1	

Problem Solving with Math Models© 2012

Unit 3 – Put Together /Take Apart Problems

PUT TOGETHER/TAKE APART--BOTH ADDENDS UNKNOWN

7. There are 5 rings in the store. Some of the rings were silver and some of the rings were gold. How many of each could there be if there were some of each?

Way#1: Draw pictures

Way#2: Solve with a table (fill in the table)

RINGS IN THE STORE	
Silver	Gold
4	
3	
2	
1	

Unit 3 – Put Together /Take Apart Problems

PUT TOGETHER/TAKE APART--BOTH ADDENDS UNKNOWN

8. Isaiah has 10 dogs. Some are brown and some are white. How many dogs could be brown? How many dogs could be white? There are some of each.

Way #1: Draw pictures

Way #2: Solve with a table (fill in the table)

DOGS	
Brown	White
9	
8	
7	
6	
5	
4	
3	
2	
1	

Problem Solving with Math Models© 2012

Unit 3 – Put Together /Take Apart Problems

CHAPTER 2 QUIZ: PUT TOGETHER/TAKE APART --BOTH ADDENDS UNKNOWN

Solve with a model:

1. John had 5 marbles. Some of the marbles are orange and some of the marbles are green. How many could there be of each color? There were some of each.

2. Brianna had 7 hair ties. Some of the hair ties were yellow and some of the hair ties were pink. How many of each color could she have? There were some of each.

Unit 3 – Put Together /Take Apart Problems

3. Justin had 8 books. Some of the books were about cars and some of the books were about sports. How many of each of the books could he have? There were some of each.

4. Sofia had 4 dresses. Some of them were short and some of them were long. How many of each could she have had? There were some of each.

Unit 3 – Put Together / Take Apart Problems

CHAPTER 3
PUT TOGETHER/TAKE APART PROBLEMS PART UNKNOWN

These types of problems are about sets of things. In them we know the total and one part of the set. We are looking for the other part of the set.

PROBLEM	John had ten apples. Five were red apples and the rest were green. How many apples were green?
MODEL	+5 (number line from 5 to 10 with five hops)
EQUATION	10 – 5 = ? 10 – 5 = 5

Unit 3 – Put Together /Take Apart Problems

PUT TOGETHER/TAKE APART - PART UNKNOWN

1. Kendra had 8 markers. Seven markers were orange and the rest were purple. How many markers were purple?

Way #1: Solve with a ten frame

Way #2: Write an equation and use a symbol for the unknown amount. Solve.

Explain your thinking:

Unit 3 – Put Together /Take Apart Problems

PUT TOGETHER/TAKE APART - PART UNKNOWN

2. Tabitha had 15 cookies. Nine cookies were chocolate chip and the rest were sugar cookies. How many were sugar cookies?

Way #1: Solve with a double ten frame

Way #2: Write an equation and use a symbol for the unknown amount. Solve.

Explain your thinking:

Put Together/Take Apart - Part Unknown

3. Simon had 50 cents. He had only 1 quarter. Name one way that he could have the rest of the money.

Way #1: Solve with a number line or drawings.

Way #2: Write an equation and use a symbol for the unknown amount. Solve.

Explain your thinking:

Unit 3 – Put Together /Take Apart Problems

PUT TOGETHER/TAKE APART - PART UNKNOWN

4. The pet store had 73 fish. Twenty-nine were rainbow fish and the rest were goldfish. How many goldfish were there?

Way#1: Solve with a number grid

1	2	3	4	5	6	7	8	9	10
11	12	13	14	15	16	17	18	19	20
21	22	23	24	25	26	27	28	29	30
31	32	33	34	35	36	37	38	39	40
41	42	43	44	45	46	47	48	49	50
51	52	53	54	55	56	57	58	59	60
61	62	63	64	65	66	67	68	69	70
71	72	73	74	75	76	77	78	79	80
81	82	83	84	85	86	87	88	89	90
91	92	93	94	95	96	97	98	99	100

Way#2: Write an equation and use a symbol for the unknown amount. Solve.

Explain your thinking:

Unit 3 – Put Together /Take Apart Problems

PUT TOGETHER/TAKE APART - PART UNKNOWN

5. Maria had 100 centimeters of string. Fifty-nine cm were yellow and the rest was green. How many cm were green?

Way#1: Solve with an open number line

Way#2: Write an equation and use a symbol for the unknown amount. Solve.

Explain your thinking:

Unit 3 – Put Together /Take Apart Problems

PUT TOGETHER/TAKE APART - PART UNKNOWN

6. Marta drew a 12-inch line. She colored 6 inches purple and the rest pink. How much did she color pink?

Way #1: Solve with a drawing of a ruler

Way #2: Write an equation and use a symbol for the unknown amount. Solve.

Explain your thinking:

Unit 3 – Put Together/Take Apart Problems

PUT TOGETHER/TAKE APART—PART UNKNOWN

7. The deli had 89 sandwiches. There were 33 turkey, 28 vegetarian and the rest were chicken. How many sandwiches were chicken?

Way #1: Solve with an open number line

Way #2: Write an equation and use a symbol for the unknown amount. Solve.

Explain your thinking:

Unit 3 – Put Together/Take Apart Problems

PUT TOGETHER/TAKE APART - PART UNKNOWN

8. The pet store had 100 fish. They had 40 beta fish, 10 rainbow fish, 20 guppies and the rest were angelfish. How many angelfish did they have?

Way #1: Solve with an open number line

Way #2: Write an equation and use a symbol for the unknown amount. Solve.

Explain your thinking:

Unit 3 – Put Together /Take Apart Problems

Chapter 3 Quiz: Put Together/Take Apart - Part Unknown

Solve with a model:

1. Sonia had 15 rings. Ten were purple and the rest were pink. How many were pink?

2. Jackson had 80 cents. He had 2 quarters and some nickels. How many nickels did he have?

Unit 3 – Put Together /Take Apart Problems

3. Kelly had 40 bracelets. Twenty were leather and the rest were plastic. How many were plastic?

4. Adrian had 100 centimeters of string. She had thirty-three cm of pink string and the rest was orange. How much orange string did she have?

Unit 3 – Put Together /Take Apart Problems

UNIT 3 TEST:
PART PART WHOLE TEST

Solve with a model:

1. Jan has 20 blue marbles, 39 pink ones, 15 rainbow ones and 10 orange ones. How many marbles does she have altogether?

2. Lucas has 100 cm of yarn. Forty-three cm of it is yellow and the rest is blue. How many cm are blue?

Unit 3 – Put Together /Take Apart Problems

3. Kelly had 5 stickers. Some were butterflies and some were dogs. She had some of each. How many of each could she have had?

4. Raul drew a 12-inch line. He colored 5 inches green and the rest blue. How much did he color blue?

UNIT 4 - Comparison Problems

CHAPTER 1
COMPARE DIFFERENCE UNKNOWN

In these problems students are comparing two or more amounts. They are comparing to find out what is the difference between the amounts. There are two versions of this type of story. One version uses the word more and one version uses the word fewer. The version with the word fewer is more difficult.

PROBLEM MORE VERSION	John had turtles. Carl had 2 turtles. How many more turtles does John have than Carl?
MODEL	John Carl ←—2——Difference is 10——12—→
EQUATION	12 - ? = 2 12 - 10 = 12

PROBLEM FEWER VERSION	Carl had 2 marbles. John had 12 marbles. How many fewer marbles does Carl have than John?
MODEL	John ●● (●●●●●●●●●●) Carl ●●
EQUATION	2 + ? = 12 2 + 10 = 12

Problem Solving with Math Models© 2012

Unit 4 – Comparison Problems

COMPARE DIFFERENCE UNKNOWN

1. Cameron has 9 posters. Danielle has 3. How many more posters does Cameron have than Danielle?

Way#1: Solve with drawings

Way#2: Use >, =, and < symbols to record the results of comparisons.

Explain your thinking:

Unit 4 – Comparison Problems

COMPARE DIFFERENCE UNKNOWN

2. Ricardo has 15 pencils. Emily has 5 pencils. How many more pencils would Emily need to have the same amount as Ricardo?

Way #1: Solve with drawings

Way #2: Use >, =, and < symbols to record the results of comparisons.

Explain your thinking:

Unit 4 – Comparison Problems

COMPARE DIFFERENCE UNKNOWN

3. The 1st grade voted on their favorite types of cold drinks. Use the data in the frequency table to make a line plot.

Favorite Cold Drinks	
Iced Tea	7
Lemonade	19
Water	32
Soda	38

Draw a line plot to represent the data

Question 1: How many people voted altogether?

Question 2: How many more people liked soda than liked lemonade?

Question 3: How many fewer people liked iced tea than liked water?

Unit 4 – Comparison Problems

COMPARE DIFFERENCE UNKNOWN

4. The 2nd grade voted on their favorite types of movies. Use the data in the frequency table to make a picture graph

Favorite Movies	
Cartoons	34
Comedies	14
Space	29
Cowboy	17

Draw a picture graph to represent the data

Question 1: How many people voted altogether?

Question 2: How many more people liked cartoons than liked cowboy movies?

Question 3: How many fewer people liked comedies than liked space movies?

Problem Solving with Math Models© 2012

Unit 4 – Comparison Problems

COMPARE DIFFERENCE UNKNOWN

5. The bakery has 55 fudge brownies. It has 10 less lemon bars. How many lemon bars does it have?

Way#1: Solve with a double number line

Way#2: Use >, =, and < symbols to record the results of comparisons.

Explain your thinking:

Unit 4 – Comparison Problems

COMPARE DIFFERENCE UNKNOWN

6. The bike shop had 18 tricycles and 42 bicycles. How many fewer tricycles did the store have than bicycles?

Way #1: Solve with a double number line

Way #2: Use >, =, and < symbols to record the results of comparisons.

Explain your thinking:

Problem Solving with Math Models© 2012

Unit 4 – Comparison Problems

COMPARE DIFFERENCE UNKNOWN

7. The 3rd grade voted on their favorite types of reptiles. Use the data in the frequency table to make a bar graph.

Favorite Reptiles	
Snakes	24
Alligators/Crocodiles	20
Lizards	39
Other	17

Draw a bar graph to represent the data

Question 1: How many people voted altogether?

Question 2: How many more people liked lizards than liked snakes?

Question 3: How many fewer people liked alligators than liked lizards?

Unit 4 – Comparison Problems

COMPARE DIFFERENCE UNKNOWN

8. Cole has 2 quarters and 3 nickels. John has 2 quarters and a dime. Who has more money? How much more money?

Way#1: Solve with a double number line or drawings

Way#2: Use >, =, and < symbols to record the results of comparisons.

Explain your thinking:

Unit 4 – Comparison Problems

CHAPTER 1 QUIZ:
COMPARE DIFFERENCE UNKNOWN PROBLEMS

Solve with a model:

1. Sue had 88 cm of string. Jessica had 59 cm of string. How much less string does Jessica have than Sue?

2. Jamal had 5 nickels and Joe had 4 dimes and 5 pennies. Who has more money? How much more money?

3. The bakery had 55 brownies and 86 lemon bars. How many more brownies would the bakery need to make to have the same amount of brownies as lemon bars?

4. Grandma made 36 oatmeal cookies and 48 chocolate chip cookies. How many more chocolate chip cookies did she make than oatmeal ones?

Unit 4 – Comparison Problems

CHAPTER 2
COMPARISON – BIGGER PART UNKNOWN

In these problems students are comparing two or more amounts. They are comparing to find out who had the bigger part. There are two versions of this type of story. One version uses the word more and one version uses the word fewer. The version with the word fewer is more difficult.

PROBLEM MORE VERSION	John has 5 more marbles than Carl. Carl has 2 marbles. How many marbles does John have?
MODEL	John — 7 total Carl
EQUATION	5 + 2 = ? 5 + 2 = 7

PROBLEM FEWER VERSION	Carl has 3 fewer marbles than John? Carl has 2 marbles. How many marbles does John have?
MODEL	Carl John 5 total
EQUATION	2 + 3 = ? 2 + 3 = 5

Unit 4 – Comparison Problems

COMPARISON – BIGGER PART UNKNOWN

1. Denver has 3 stars. Ethan has 5 more than he does. How many stars does Ethan have?

Way #1: Solve with drawings

Way #2: Solve with numbers

Explain your thinking:

Unit 4 – Comparison Problems

COMPARISON – BIGGER PART UNKNOWN

2. Lance has 6 apples. Aiden has 4 more than he does. How many apples does Aiden have?

Way #1: Solve with drawings

Way #2: Solve with numbers

Explain your thinking:

Unit 4 – Comparison Problems

COMPARISON – BIGGER PART UNKNOWN

3. Emily has 6 marbles. She has 6 less than George. How many marbles does George have?

Way #1: Solve with drawings

Way #2: Solve with numbers

Explain your thinking:

Problem Solving with Math Models© 2012

Unit 4 – Comparison Problems

COMPARISON – BIGGER PART UNKNOWN

4. The toy store has 55 soccer balls. There are 30 more basketballs than soccer balls. How many basketballs are there?

Way#1: Solve with a double number line

Way#2: Solve with numbers

Explain your thinking:

Unit 4 – Comparison Problems

COMPARISON – BIGGER PART UNKNOWN

5. Mike has 2 quarters and a dime. Luke has 20 more cents than Mike. How much money does Luke have?

Way #1: Solve with a double number line

Way #2: Solve with numbers

Explain your thinking:

Unit 4 – Comparison Problems

COMPARISON – BIGGER PART UNKNOWN

6. Carla has 3 quarters. Benji has 1 more quarter than Carla. How much money does Benji have?

Way #1: Solve with a double number line

Way #2: Solve with numbers

Explain your thinking:

Unit 4 – Comparison Problems

COMPARISON – BIGGER PART UNKNOWN

7. Jessica had 48 cm of string. Mary had 12 more cm than Jessica. How much string did Mary have?

Way #1: Solve with a double number line

Way #2: Solve with numbers

Explain your thinking:

Unit 4 – Comparison Problems

COMPARISON – BIGGER PART UNKNOWN

8. The zoo has 80 stuffed elephants. They have 10 more giraffes than elephants. How many giraffes do they have?

Way #1: Solve with a double number line

Way #2: Solve with numbers

Explain your thinking:

Unit 4 – Comparison Problems

CHAPTER 2 QUIZ:
COMPARE BIGGER PART UNKNOWN

Solve with a model:

1. John has 57 marbles. Steve has 23 more marbles than John. How many marbles does Steve have?

2. Lucy has 12 bracelets. She has 3 fewer bracelets than Chloe. How many bracelets does Chloe have?

Problem Solving with Math Models© 2012

Unit 4 – Comparison Problems

3. Raul has 3 quarters and 2 dimes. Miguel has that amount plus a nickel more. How much money does Miguel have?

4. Lucy jumped 24 inches. Mike jumped 12 more inches than she did. How far did Mike jump?

Unit 4 – Comparison Problems

CHAPTER 3
COMPARISON – SMALLER PART UNKNOWN

In these problems students are comparing two or more amounts. They are comparing to find out who has the smaller amount. There are two versions of this type of story. One version uses the word more and one version uses the word fewer. The version with the word fewer is more difficult.

PROBLEM MORE VERSION	John had 4 more marbles than Carl. John had 5 marbles. How many marbles did Carl have?
MODEL	John ● ●● ●● Carl ●
	5 - 4 = ? 5 – 4 = 1

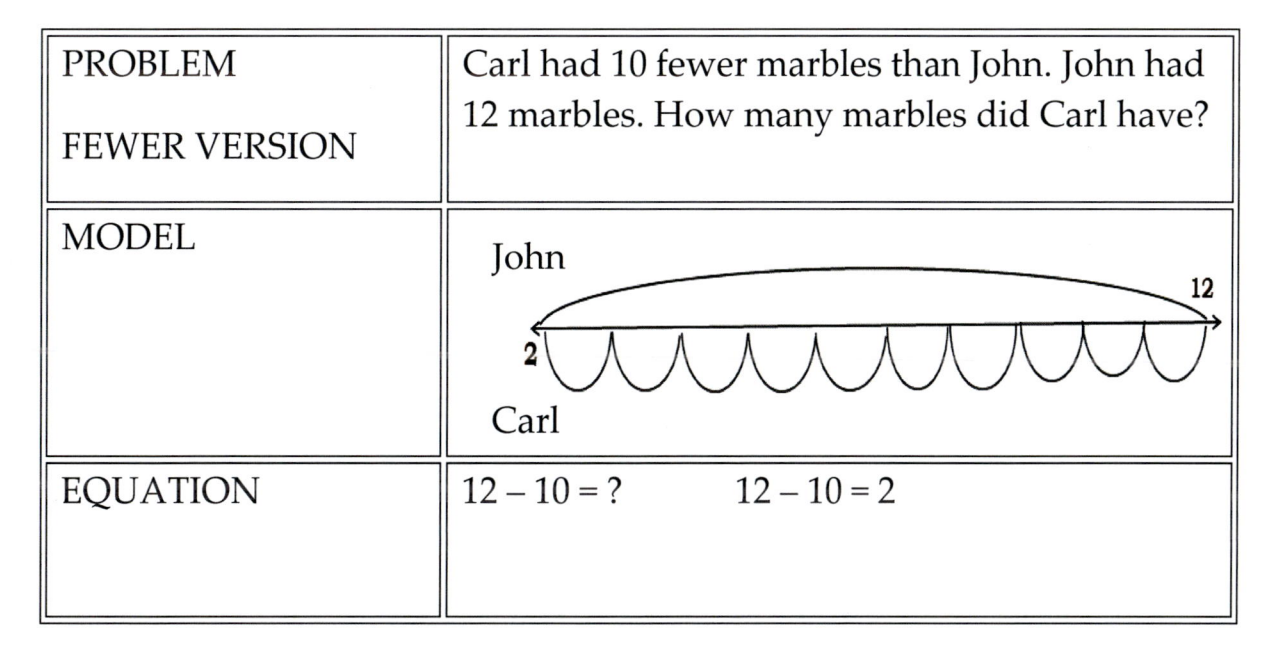

PROBLEM FEWER VERSION	Carl had 10 fewer marbles than John. John had 12 marbles. How many marbles did Carl have?
MODEL	John ⌒⌢⌢⌢⌢⌢⌢ 12 2 Carl
EQUATION	12 – 10 = ? 12 – 10 = 2

Unit 4 – Comparison Problems

COMPARISON – SMALLER PART UNKNOWN

1. Luke has 7 toy boats. Julian has 2 less than he does. How many toy boats does Julian have?

Way #1: Solve with drawings

Way #2: Solve with numbers

Explain your thinking:

Unit 4 – Comparison Problems

COMPARISON – SMALLER PART UNKNOWN

2. Amanda has 9 chapter books. Melissa has 3 less than she does. How many chapter books does Melissa have?

Way#1: Solve with drawings

Way#2: Solve with numbers

Explain your thinking:

Unit 4 – Comparison Problems

COMPARISON – SMALLER PART UNKNOWN

3. Jennifer has 8 dimes. Isabella has 1 less dime than she does. How much money does Isabella have?

Way #1: Solve with an open number line or drawings

Way #2: Solve with numbers

Explain your thinking:

Unit 4 – Comparison Problems

COMPARISON – SMALLER PART UNKNOWN

4. The bookstore has 22 butterfly bookmarkers. It has 15 less sports bookmarkers. How many sports bookmarkers does it have?

Way #1: Solve with drawings

Way #2: Solve with numbers

Explain your thinking:

Problem Solving with Math Models© 2012

Unit 4 – Comparison Problems

COMPARISON – SMALLER PART UNKNOWN

5. Jessica has 92 cm of string. Lucy has 30 cm less than she does. How much string does Lucy have?

Way #1: Solve with a double number line

Way #2: Solve with numbers

Explain your thinking:

Unit 4 – Comparison Problems

COMPARISON – SMALLER PART UNKNOWN

6. The bakery made 67 lemon cookies and 18 fewer cherry ones than lemon ones for the festival. How many cherry cookies did the bakery make?

Way#1: Solve with a double number line

Way#2: Solve with numbers

Explain your thinking:

Problem Solving with Math Models© 2012

Unit 4 – Comparison Problems

COMPARISON – SMALLER PART UNKNOWN

7. The craft store sold 50 yards of Material A and 30 yards less of Material B. How many yards of Material B did it sell?

Way #1: Solve with a double number line

Way #2: Solve with numbers

Explain your thinking:

Unit 4 – Comparison Problems

COMPARISON – SMALLER PART UNKNOWN

8. Kiyana had 4 dimes and 2 nickels. Justine had 8 cents less than she did. How much money did Justine have?

Way #1: Solve with an open number line or drawings

Way #2: Use >, =, and < symbols to record the results of comparisons.

Explain your thinking:

Unit 4 – Comparison Problems

CHAPTER 3 QUIZ:
COMPARE SMALLER UNKNOWN PROBLEMS

Solve with a model:

1. Mary had 70 rings. She had 20 more rings than Susan. How many rings did Susan have?

2. Ricardo had 72 computer games. He had 25 more computer games than Luke. How many computer games did Luke have?

Unit 4 – Comparison Problems

3. Jamal had 23 green hockey sticks, 14 orange hockey sticks, and 34 blue ones. Mike had 10 less hockey sticks than he did. How many hockey sticks did Mike have?

4. Out of 4 jumps, Luke jumped a total of 9 ft. Marcus jumped 2 feet less than he did. How many feet did Marcus jump?

Problem Solving with Math Models© 2012

Unit 4 Test: Compare Problems

Solve with a model:

1. Sue had 5 mangos. Nathan had 10. How many fewer mangos did Sue have than Nathan?

2. The class took a vote on their favorite flavors of bubblegum. Use the data in the frequency table to make a picture graph.

Favorite Flavors of Bubblegum	
Traditional	12
Fruity	10
Mint	3
Other	2

Draw a bar graph to represent the data

Question 1: How many people voted altogether?

Question 2: How many people liked traditional flavored gum than mint flavored gum?

Question 3: Write a question about this data

Problem Solving with Math Models© 2012

3. Juan had 10 dimes. He had 2 more dimes than Kirk. How much money did Kirk have?

4. Mary had 27 stickers. Kayla had 20 stickers. How many more stickers did Mary have than Kayla?

5. Kelly had 3 fewer yards of yarn than Lela. Kelly had 7 yards of yarn. How many yards of yarn did Lela have?

6. The 2nd grade voted on their favorite types of vegetables. Use the data in the frequency table to make a picture graph

Favorite Types of Vegetables	
Potatoes	35
Spinach	24
Carrots	19
Other	10

Draw a picture graph to represent the data

Question 1: How many people voted altogether?

Question 2: How many more people liked potatoes than spinach?

Question 3: How many fewer people liked carrots than spinach?

7. The 2nd grade voted on their favorite types of movies. Use the data in the frequency table to make a line plot

Favorite Ways to Eat a Potato	
Baked	26
French Fries	40
Home Fries	20
Other	14

Draw a line plot to represent the data

Question 1: How many people voted altogether?

Question 2: How many more people liked French fries than home fries?

Question 3: How many fewer people liked home fries than liked baked potatoes?

Unit 4 – Comparison Problems

8. Marcos had 5 fewer video games than Tom. Tom had 7 video games. How many marbles did Marcos have?

9. Alan had 10 fewer packs of cards than Maria. He had 70 packs of cards. How many packs did she have?

10. Lela had 24 green hair ribbons, 24 pink hair ribbons and 34 blue hair ribbons. Kate had 10 more than Lela. How many hair ribbons did Kate have?

Problem Solving with Math Models© 2012

UNIT 5 - Multi-Step Problems

CHAPTER 1
MULTISTEP WORD PROBLEMS

There are 5 types of CCSS two-step problems. In these problems, either the steps involve the same operation, two different operations, or a mixture of different problem types. Throughout this chapter, we will practice each type.

Multi-Step/Different Operations

PROBLEM	There were 5 comic books and 2 sports books on the shelf. Susie put 2 more comic books on the shelf. How many books are there on the shelf now?
MODEL	[bracket diagram with ? above three boxes: "5 comic books", "2 sports books", "2 more comic books"]
EQUATIONS	5 + 2 = 7 7 + 2 = 9

Problem Solving with Math Models© 2012

Unit 5 – Multi-Step Problems

PROBLEM	There were 5 books on the table. John took 3 books. Sue put 7 more books on the table. How many books are on the table now?
MODEL	
EQUATIONS	5 - 3 = 2 2 + 7 = 9

Multi-Step/Different Problem Types

PROBLEM	Sue had 5 candies. Terri had 2 more candies than Sue. How many candies did they have altogether?
MODEL	
EQUATIONS	5 + 2 = 7 5 + 7 = 12

Unit 5 – Multi-Step Problems

Multi-Step/Mixed Problem Types

PROBLEM	There were 5 comic books and some sports books on a shelf. There were 10 books altogether. Sue put 2 more sports books on the shelf. How many sports books are there now?
MODEL	(number line showing +5 Comics, +5 Sports, 10, +2, 12)
EQUATIONS	5 + ? = 10 5 + 5 = 10 10 + 2 = 7

Multi-Step/Different Operations

PROBLEM	There were 3 red marbles and some green marbles on the table. There were 5 marbles in all. Then Sue put some more green marbles on the table and now there are 10 green marbles on the table. How many green marbles did Sue put on the table?
MODEL	Red ● ●● Green ●● + ●●●●●●●●
EQUATIONS	3 + ? = 5 2 + ? = 10 2 + 8 = 10

168　　　　　　　　　　　　　　　　　　Problem Solving with Math Models© 2012

Unit 5 – Multi-Step Problems

MULTI-STEP/SAME OPERATION

Solve with a model:

1. Mrs. Quezada had 2 yards of green yarn. Then she bought 4 yards of yellow yarn. Her mother gave her 10 yards of pink yarn. How many yards of yarn does she have altogether now?

2. Melanie had 50 marbles. Her brother gave her 20 more. Then, her mom gave her 15 more. How many does she have altogether now?

Problem Solving with Math Models© 2012

Unit 5 – Multi-Step Problems

3. Tony had 15 stickers. He gave 5 to his brother. He gave 5 to his sister. Now, how many does he have left?

4. Raul had 55 cents. He gave his brother a quarter. He gave his sister a dime. How much money does he have left now?

Unit 5 – Multi-Step Problems

MULTI-STEP/MIXED OPERATIONS

Solve with a model:

1. Dan had 29 magazines. His brother had 10 less than he did. How many do they have altogether?

2. Carlos had 34 baseball hats. His brother had 10 more than he did. How many do they have altogether?

Unit 5 – Multi-Step Problems

3. There were 5 blue marbles and some green marbles in the bag. There were 15 marbles altogether. John put 4 more green marbles in the bag. How many green marbles are in the bag now?

4. Tony had 7 toy cars and some toy trucks in the toy box. He had 20 toy vehicles in the box altogether. Then, he put 5 more trucks in the toy box. How many toy trucks does he have altogether now?

Unit 5 – Multi-Step Problems

5. In the ball box there were 8 soccer balls and some baseballs. All total there were 12 balls in the box. Then Tom put some more baseballs in the box. Now, there are 7 baseballs. How many baseballs did Tom put in the box?

6. In the cookie jar there were 12 oatmeal cookies and some chocolate chip cookies. All total there were 20 cookies in the cookie jar. Then, Mrs. Mabel put some more chocolate chip cookies in the jar. Now, there are 15 chocolate chip cookies in the jar. How many chocolate chip cookies did Mrs. Mabel put in the jar?

Unit 5 – Multi-Step Problems

7. There were 5 brown ties and 7 green ties in the display window at the store. Tom added 4 pink ties and 3 blue ones to the display. How many ties are in the display window altogether?

8. There were 15 green frogs on the log. There were 10 fewer blue frogs on the log. How many frogs are there altogether on the log?

Unit 5 – Multi-Step Problems

UNIT 5 TEST: MULTI-STEP WORD PROBLEMS

Solve with a model:

1. Jane had 15 stickers. Eight were animal stickers and the rest were doll stickers. Then, her sister gave her 5 more doll stickers. How many doll stickers does Jane have altogether now?

2. There were 7 blue towels and some green towels in the bag. There were 10 towels altogether in the bag. Michael put some more green towels in the bag and now there are a total of 8 green towels. How many green towels did Michael put in the bag?

Unit 5 – Multi-Step Problems

3. John had 15 candies. He gave his brother 2 and his sister 3. His mom gave him 7 more candies. How many candies does he have now?

4. James had 4 dimes. His sister gave him 2 quarters. His mother gave him 2 nickels. He gave his other sister 1 quarter. How much does he have left?

Final Word Problem Test
Second Grade

NAME:

DATE:

Solve the Problems. Show your thinking. Draw a picture, use a number line or make a table.

1. Claire had 8 nickels. She got 4 more for her birthday. How much money does she have altogether now?

2. Kanye had 9 toy cars. He got some more for his birthday. Now he has 18. How many did he get for his birthday?

Final Word Problem Test

3. Lucy had some money. She got 3 quarters and a dime for her birthday. Now she has $1.00. How much money did she have in the beginning?

4. Raul had 100 feet of wood. He made several shelves and used 86 feet. How many feet does he have left?

Final Word Problem Test

5. Maya had 95 cm of string. She used some of it. Now she has 27 cm left. How much did she use?

6. Jennifer had some money. She spent a quarter at the store. She gave 2 dimes to her sister. She has 55 cents left. How much did she have in the beginning?

Final Word Problem Test

7. Marcus has 27 car stickers and 37 animal ones. How many stickers does he have altogether?

8. Mark had 10 marbles. Some were brown and some were orange. How many of each could he have? He had some of both.

Final Word Problem Test

9. Larry had 35 books. Twenty were about tigers and the rest were about lions. How many books were about lions?

10. Mini gave out 47 purple rings and 67 pink ones at her party. How many more pink ones did she give than purple ones?

Problem Solving with Math Models© 2012

Final Word Problem Test

11. Tom had 57 animal stickers and 47 truck stickers. How many fewer truck stickers did he have than animal ones?

12. Jose had 10 more markers than Carlos. Carlos has 25 markers. How many markers does Jose have?

13. Kate has 3 fewer rings than Kiyana. Kate has 12 rings. How many rings does Kiyana have?

14. James had 4 fewer trophies than his brother. His brother has 28 trophies. How many trophies does James have?

Final Word Problem Test

15. Shakhira has 5 more sweaters than Samantha. Shakhira has 10 sweaters. How many sweaters does Samantha have?

16. There were 15 apples on the table. Mom put 8 more on the table. Dad put 7 more on the table. How many apples are on the table now?

Final Word Problem Test

17. There were 20 biscuits on the table. Grandma ate 2 of them. Cousin Dave put 5 more on the table. Clark ate 3 of them. How many biscuits are on the table now?

18. Sue had 25 pieces of gum. Tom had 2 more pieces than she did. How many pieces do they have altogether?

Final Word Problem Test

19. There were 7 squirrels and some butterflies in the tree. There were 17 animals altogether. Then, 4 more butterflies landed on the tree. How many butterflies are on the tree now?

20. There were 8 butterflies and some beetles on the flower. There were 10 insects on the flower altogether. Then, some more beetles flew onto the flower. Now there are 16 beetles on the flower. How many more beetles flew onto the flower?

Final Word Problem Test

21. There were 100 potato chips on the table. John ate 20 of them. Clark ate 30 of them. Marta ate 25 of them. How many were left?

Final Word Problem Test

22. The Kindergarten students voted on their favorite types of stuffed animals. Use the data in the frequency table to make a line plot.

Favorite Types of Stuffed Animals	
Bears	40
Rabbits	30
TV/Cartoon Character	20
Other	10

Draw a line plot to represent the data

Question 1: How many people voted altogether?

Question 2: How many more people liked bears than liked rabbits?

Question 3: How many fewer people liked cartoon characters than liked rabbits?

Final Word Problem Test

23. The 2nd grade students voted on their favorite types of hot drinks. Use the data in the frequency table to make a picture graph.

Favorite Types of Drinks	
Apple cider	30
Hot chocolate	40
Tea	20
Other	10

Draw a picture graph to represent the data

Question 1: How many people voted altogether?

Question 2: How many more people liked hot chocolate than liked tea?

Question 3: How many fewer people liked other things than apple cider?

Final Word Problem Test

24. The 4th grade students voted on their favorite types of sports. Use the data in the frequency table to make a bar graph.

Favorite Types of Sports	
Baseball	25
Football	15
Soccer	35
Other	20

Draw a bar graph to represent the data

Question 1: How many people voted altogether?

Question 2: How many more people liked soccer than baseball?

Question 3: How many fewer people liked football than liked soccer?

ANSWER KEY

Unit 1 – Add to Problems

Chapter 1: Add to Result Unknown Problems

1. 10 marbles
2. 15 markers
3. 89 flower stamps
4. 30; 17
5. 29; 20
6. 73 cents
7. 62 cm of string
8. 29; 15

Chapter 1 Quiz: Add to Results Unknown

1. 17 marbles
2. 23 rings
3. 12 action figures
4. 28 altogether; 16

Chapter 2: Add to Change Unknown Problems

1. 4 toy airplanes
2. 10 cookies
3. 4 in. of string
4. 11 toy cars
5. 16 cents
6. 30; 7
7. 2 dimes
8. 26; 7

Chapter 2 Quiz: Add to Change Unknown Problem

1. 5 stickers
2. 15 cents
3. 21 cupcakes
4. 8 in. of string

Chapter 3: Add to Start Unknown

1. 5 gummy bears
2. 9 blocks
3. 76 cookies
4. 49 lollipops
5. 25 pencils
6. 5 cents
7. 2 in. of string
8. 28 stuffed animals

Chapter 3 Quiz: Add to Start Unknown Problems

1. 7 bracelets
2. 12 steaks
3. 25 cents
4. 16 pizzas

UNIT 1 TEST: ADDITION PROBLEMS

1. 84 dollhouses
2. 70 cents
3. 52 cakes
4. 30 baseball trading cards

Problem Solving with Math Models© 2012

ANSWER KEY

Unit 2 – Take From Problems

Chapter 1: Take From Result Unknown

1. 3 apples
2. 9 crayons
3. 15 cents
4. 72 butterfly stamps
5. 7 inches
6. 69 stickers
7. 41 lemon trees
8. 17 in. of string

Chapter 1 Quiz: Take From Result Unknown Problems

1. 52 cents
2. 63 seashells
3. 2 in.
4. 29 rings

Chapter 2: Take From Change Unknown Problems

1. 5 strawberries
2. 7 grapes
3. 80 chocolate bars
4. 56 packs of gum
5. 53 cents
6. 85 bunnies
7. 29 in.
8. 79 magazines

Chapter 2 Quiz: Take From Change Unknown Problems

1. 63 cents
2. 36 seashells
3. 61 cm.
4. 50 rings

Chapter 3: Take From Start Unknown Problems

1. 9 pencils
2. 20 gummy bears
3. 116 waffle cones
4. 64 cm.
5. 10 in.
6. 80 action figures
7. 69 cookies
8. 20 bracelets

Chapter 3 Quiz: Take From Start Unknown Problems

1. 80 cents
2. 11 in.
3. 84 brownies
4. 100 tires

UNIT 2 TEST: TAKE FROM PROBLEMS

1. 32 marbles
2. 100 cm.
3. 24 cents
4. 75 stickers

ANSWER KEY

Unit 3 – Put Together/Take Apart

Chapter 1: Put Together/Take Apart— Whole Unknown Problems

1. 10 pets
2. 19 hats
3. 70 cents
4. 91 stickers
5. 27; 10
6. 29; 14
7. 31; 20
8. 93 balls

Chapter 1 Quiz: Put Together/Take Apart—Whole Unknown Problems

1. 12 cm
2. 90 cents
3. 65 balls
4. 32; 22

Chapter 2: Put Together/Take Apart— Both Addends Unknown Problems

1. Skirts

Pink	Green
7	1
6	2
5	3
4	4
3	5
2	6
1	7

2. Students in Class

Girls	Boys
4	1
3	2
2	3
1	4

3. Slices of Pizza

Pepperoni	Plain Cheese
5	1
4	2
3	3
2	4
1	5

Answer Key

Unit 3 – Put Together/Take Apart

4. Bears

Brown	Black
3	1
2	2
1	3

5. Cats

Black	Striped
2	1
1	2

6. Books

Airplanes	Cars
4	1
3	2
2	3
1	4

7. Rings in the store

Silver	Gold
4	1
3	2
2	3
1	4

8. Dogs

Brown	White
9	1
8	2
7	3
6	4
5	5
4	6
3	7
2	8
1	9

Chapter 2 Quiz: Put Together/Take Apart—Both Addends Unknown

1. Marbles

Orange	Green
4	1
3	2
2	3
1	4

2. Hair Ties

Yellow	Pink
6	1
5	2
4	3
3	4
2	5
1	6

ANSWER KEY

Unit 3 – Put Together/Take Apart

3. Books	
Cars	Sports
7	1
6	2
5	3
4	4
3	5
2	6
1	7

4. Dresses	
Short	Long
3	1
2	2
1	3

Chapter 3: Put Together/Take Apart— Part Unknown Problems

1. 1 marker
2. 6 sugar cookies
3. 2 dimes, 1 nickel; answers will vary
4. 44 goldfish
5. 41 cm.
6. 6 in.
7. 28 chicken sandwiches
8. 30 angelfish

Chapter 3 Quiz: Put Together/Take Apart—Part Unknown Problems

1. 5 pink rings
2. 6 nickels
3. 20 plastic bracelets
4. 67 cm.

Unit 3 Test

1. 84 marbles
2. 57 cm
3.

Butterflies	Dogs
4	1
3	2
2	3
1	4

4. 7 in.

Problem Solving with Math Models© 2012

Answer Key

Unit 4 – Comparison/Difference Problems

Chapter 1: Compare Difference Unknown Problems

1. 6 more posters
2. 10 more pencils
3. 96; 19; 25
4. 94; 17;15
5. 45 lemon bars
6. 24 fewer tricycles
7. 100; 15;19
8. Cole; 5 cents

Chapter 1 Quiz: Compare Difference Unknown Problems

1. 29 cm. less
2. Joe; 20 cents
3. 31 more brownies
4. 12 more chocolate chip cookies

Chapter 2: Comparison—Bigger Part Unknown Problems

1. 8 stars
2. 10 apples
3. 12 marbles
4. 85 basketballs
5. 80 cents
6. $1
7. 60 cm.
8. 90 giraffes

Chapter 2 Quiz: Comparison—Bigger Part Unknown Problems

1. 80 marbles
2. 15 bracelets
3. $1
4. 36 in.

Chapter 3: Comparison—Smaller Part Unknown Problems

1. 5 toy boats
2. 6 chapter books
3. 70 cents
4. 7 sports bookmarks
5. 62 cm.
6. 49 cherry cookies
7. 20 yds.
8. 42 cents

Chapter 3 Quiz: Comparison Smaller Unknown Problems

1. 50 rings
2. 47 computer games
3. 61 hockey sticks
4. 7 ft.

UNIT 4 TEST: COMPARE PROBLEMS

1. 5 fewer mangos
2. 27;9
3. 80 cents
4. 7 more stickers
5. 10 yds.
6. 88; 11; 5
7. 100; 20; 6
8. 2 video games
9. 80 packs of cards
10. 92 hair ribbons

ANSWER KEY

Unit 5 – Two-Step Problems

Multi-step/Same Operation Problems

1. 16 yds.
2. 85 marbles
3. 5 stickers
4. 20 cents

Multi-step/Mixed Operations Problems

1. 48 magazines altogether
2. 78 baseball hats
3. 14 green marbles
4. 18 trucks
5. 3 baseballs
6. 7 chocolate chip cookies
7. 19 ties altogether
8. 20 frogs altogether

UNIT 5 TEST: Multi-Step Word Problems

1. 12 doll stickers
2. 5 green towels
3. 17 candies
4. 75 cents

FINAL WORD PROBLEM TEST

1. 60 cents
2. 9 toy cars
3. 15 cents
4. 14 ft.
5. 68 cm
6. $1
7. 64 stickers

8. Marbles	
Brown	Orange
9	1
8	2
7	3
6	4
5	5
4	6
3	7
2	8
1	9

9. 15 books about lions
10. 20 more pink rings
11. 10 fewer truck stickers
12. 35 markers
13. 15 rings
14. 24 trophies
15. 5 sweaters
16. 30 apples
17. 20 biscuits
18. 27 pieces of gum
19. 14 butterflies
20. 14 beetles
21. 25 chips
22. 100;10; 10
23. 100;20;20
24. 95;10;20

Problem Solving with Math Models© 2012

REFERENCES

Carpenter, T., Fennema, E., Franke, M., Levi, L., & Empson, S. (1999). *Children's Mathematics: Cognitively Guided Instruction*. Portsmouth, NH: Heinemann.

Charles, R.   *Solving Word Problems: Developing Students' Quantitative Reasoning Abilities* http://assets.pearsonschool.com/asset_mgr/legacy/200931/Problem%20Solving%20Monograph_24324_1.pdf

Common Core Standards Writing Team (Bill McCullum, lead author). (2012, June 23). *Progressions for the common core state standards in mathematics: Geometry (draft)*. Retrieved from: www.commoncoretools.wordpress.com.

Common Core Standards Writing Team (Bill McCullum, lead author). (2012, June 23). *Progressions for the common core state standards in mathematics: Geometric measurement (draft)*. Retrieved from: www.commoncoretools.wordpress.com.

Common Core Standards Writing Team (Bill McCullum, lead author). (2011, June 20). *Progressions for the common core state standards in mathematics: K-3, Categorical data; Grades 2-5, Measurement Data (draft)*. Retrieved from: www.commoncoretools.wordpress.com.

Common Core Standards Writing Team (Bill McCullum, lead author). (2011, May 29). *Progressions for the common core state standards in mathematics: K, Counting and cardinality; K-5, operations and algebraic thinking (draft)*. Retrieved from: www.commoncoretools.wordpress.com.

Common Core Standards Writing Team (Bill McCullum, lead author). (2011, April 7). *Progressions for the common core state standards in mathematics: K-5, Number and operations in base ten (draft)*. Retrieved from: www.commoncoretools.wordpress.com.

Common Core Standards Writing Team (Bill McCullum, lead author). (2011, July 12). *Progressions for the common core state standards in mathematics: 3-5 Number and operations - fractions (draft)*. Retrieved from: www.commoncoretools.wordpress.com.

Peterson, P. L., Carpenter, T. P., & Loef, M. (1989). *Teachers' Pedagogical Content Beliefs in Mathematics*. Cognition and Instruction, Vol. 6, No. 1, pp. 1-40.

Made in the USA
Lexington, KY
22 August 2015